"This is an uplifting and valuable book for anyone who has been wondering how they might create more happiness in their life. The authors' ingeniously practical advice is to identify a life purpose and start a practice of engaging in simple spiritual practices. From the onset, it is very clear that this is not a book about spiritual beliefs or a particular belief system. Instead, the book uses new and proven psychological principles to help seekers identify a unique life purpose for themselves, live from the heart with intention, and deal with barriers to spiritual practice with compassion. Although the book is very practical, it is by no means superficial. It does not shy away from 'deeper issues' such as impermanence, finding a state of grace—that beautiful state of calm contentment—and bringing spirit into daily life.

By focusing on practice rather than theory or philosophy, the authors endeavor to help readers achieve a goal that many readers might have always viewed as too lofty or unachievable. This book provides hope and gives actionable advice in a personally meaningful area where really concrete and useful information is often hard to come by. I agree with the promise at the end of the book that the practices learned in this book will help readers keep Spirit alive—'in you and through you.'"

—**Georg H. Eifert, PhD**, Chapman University professor emeritus of psychology, and coauthor of *The Mindfulness and Acceptance Workbook for Anxiety*

"Get ready for a unique experience with spirituality. There are plenty of spiritual books preaching what to believe. This book defines spirituality as the process of 'doing' rather than the process of 'believing'. The authors focus on our behavior as the expression of our spirituality. So rather than 'talk' or argue about different faiths—who is right or wrong—this book is about helping you to use your spirituality as guidelines for making daily choices and acting in valued directions. The book presents fresh definitions of spirituality followed by practical guidelines, along with how to deal with obstacles while moving in valued directions, and finally a section helping the reader with a deeper understanding how spirituality can be expressed in daily life— for example, with compassion. The authors present you with lots of practical exercises. One I particularly like was called 'Morning Intention,' which combines a morning routine like making tea with a reminder of a valued intention for the day, as a way of preparing for valued living. Today, most psychotherapists or people dealing with people are including spirituality, and this book will provide you with a great palette of concepts and ways to practice doing that."

—**JoAnne Dahl, PhD**, professor in the department of psychology at Uppsala University in Uppsala, Sweden; licensed psychologist; psychotherapist; peer-reviewed acceptance and commitment therapy (ACT) trainer; and Association for Contextual Behavioral Science fellow

T0385191

"This rare and uniquely practical book offers enormous wisdom and guidance for anyone—spiritual or not, religious or not—seeking a deeper sense of meaning, purpose, and joy in their lives. *The New Happiness* will awaken you to your inner truth, your purpose in being here, and help you create the conditions for genuine happiness on your life journey."

> —**John P. Forsyth, PhD**, professor, and coauthor of *Anxiety Happens* and *The Mindfulness and Acceptance Workbook for Anxiety*

"In a world full of loss, fear, and uncertainty, working to find our deepest purpose through connecting to inner wisdom and our spiritual core is of utmost importance; it is the path to wiser choices and a fulfilling life. In Matthew McKay and Jeffrey Wood's book, the reader is guided both on a spiritual journey designed to create awareness to choice, and to great clarity about personal values in the service of growth and sustaining a spiritual environment—leading us to our true meaning. In this short but beautiful, wildly painful, blissfully amazing life, *The New Happiness* is a welcome promise for spiritual development and connection to love and all that matters in life."

> —**Robyn D. Walser, PhD**, author of *The Heart of ACT*, coauthor of *Learning ACT* and *The Mindful Couple*, and assistant professor at the University of California, Berkeley

The
New
Happiness

Practices *for* Spiritual Growth
and
Living *with* Intention

Matthew McKay, PhD & Jeffrey C. Wood, PsyD

REVEAL PRESS

AN IMPRINT OF NEW HARBINGER PUBLICATIONS

Therapists: Download a free ten-week protocol for a Post-Trauma Growth and Wisdom group, drawing on the principles and practices explored in *The New Happiness*, at http://www.newharbinger.com/43379.

Publisher's Note

Distributed in Canada by Raincoast Books

Copyright © 2019 by Matthew McKay and Jeffrey Wood
                Reveal Press
                An imprint of New Harbinger Publications, Inc.
                5674 Shattuck Avenue
                Oakland, CA 94609
                www.newharbinger.com

Cover design by Amy Shoup

Interior design by Michele Waters-Kermes

Acquired by Catharine Meyers

Edited by Ken Knabb

All Rights Reserved

Library of Congress Cataloging-in-Publication Data on file

21   20   19

10   9   8   7   6   5   4   3   2   1   First Printing

For Jordan

—Matt

For Buckley and Zoey, may you both find grace and happiness.

—Jeff

Contents

Foreword

In the mid-1990s, I was involved with a review of the scientific data on religion, spirituality, and health funded by the Templeton Foundation. William Miller, best known for his work on addictions and on Motivational Interviewing, chaired the effort, which examined mental health and physical health in many areas. The panels were catholic (with a small "c"), including behavioral and physical scientists who were atheists, agnostics, and believers in a variety of religions.

It was not hard for the review panels to reach a consensus. The scientific data were surprisingly strong in every area of health we examined: spiritual involvement predicted positive health outcomes more than virtually any other demographic variable we had data on. But neither belief per se, nor the simple social involvement and support found in community, explained the effect. Instead, the key appeared to be regular practice: actions people engaged in because of their spiritual benefits.[i]

Research in this area has continued and even ballooned in recent years.[ii] The basic findings have only strengthened. Religious *belief* can have positive or negative effects,[iii] but spiritual and religious *practice* appears to be consistently helpful, leading even to a very notable decrease in death rates.[iv]

---

i   To my knowledge, these findings were only published in a limited way. They can be found in W. R. Miller and M. E. Bennett's "Toward Better Research on Spirituality and Health: The Templeton Panels," *Spiritual and Religious Issues in Behavior Change 10* (1997): 3-4.

ii   Examples include H. G. Koenig's "Religion, Spirituality, and Health: A Review and Update," *Advances in Mind-Body Medicine 29* (3) (2015): 19-26; or H. G. Koenig, D. E. King, and V. B. Carson's *Handbook of Religion and Health*, 2nd ed. (New York: Oxford University Press, 2012).

iii   For example, disease progresses among those believing in a condemning, judgmental God [see G. Ironson et al., "View of God as Benevolent and Forgiving or Punishing and Judgmental Predicts HIV Disease Progression," *Journal of Behavioral Medicine 34* (2011): 414-425]; and spiritual struggles are toxic to mental health [see K. M. McConnell, et al., "Examining the Links Between Spiritual Struggles and Symptoms of Psychopathology in a National Sample," *Journal of Clinical Psychology 62* (MONTH 2006): 1469-1484.]

iv   R. F. Gillum, D. E. King, T. O. Obisesan, T. O., and H. G. Koenig, "Frequency of Attendance at Religious Services and Mortality in a U.S. National Cohort," *Annals of Epidemiology 18* (MONTH 2008): 124-129.

At the same time, however, religious participation is declining. Even those with a religious affiliation are going to a church, mosque, or temple less often, and the number of people without any religious affiliation is soaring, from 5 percent of adults forty-five years ago to 25 percent today.[v] Clearly there is a need for spiritual practices to emerge and flourish independent of religious affiliation or church attendance.

The New Happiness sits right inside that gap, offering a clear path to spiritual practice that fits with but does not demand belief in God. In fact, the practices this book describes and systematically teaches do not demand particular beliefs of any kind. For example, after teaching the reader to seek wisdom within, it encourages the exploration of spiritual guidance from entities without—but suggests that the reader could focus on entities as broad as the universe itself if they wish.

The authors encourage readers to explore their own spiritual world with step-by-step exercises that build on one another with unusual clarity and a gentle sense of calm guidance. Each practice taught here comports with what science shows of the helpful impact of acceptance, values work, mindfulness, compassion, atonement, prayerful guidance, and more. But the reader's own experience remains paramount. *The New Happiness* asks only that readers try these exercises and practices and see what happens in their own lives as a result.

The New Happiness gives you tools to cultivate a values- and awareness-based form of happiness that is available to us all. It is a kind of human thriving that goes far beyond "happiness" in an emotional sense, and science shows us that spiritual practice fosters it.

I personally think that this kind of thriving is exactly what's needed in the modern world. You do not need to believe—not even in "spirit"—to explore spiritual practices and their benefits. But since these benefits come from regular practice, there is only one thing left to do.

Let's begin.

Steven C. Hayes
Foundation Professor of Psychology
University of Nevada, Reno

---

v   See M. Lipka's "A Closer Look at America's Rapidly Growing Religious 'Nones,'" (Pew Research Center, May 15, 2015); or M. Hout, C. S. Fischer, and M. A. Chaves's *More Americans Have No Religious Preference: Key Finding from the 2012 General Social Survey* (Berkeley, CA: University of California, Berkeley Institute for the Study of Societal Issues, 2013).

Introduction

Every moment of your life is a spiritual opportunity—an occasion to strengthen your connection with your own inner wisdom, other people, and the universal truth that transcends time and space. For some people, "spirituality" implies a belief in God, gods, or an afterlife, but it doesn't have to. In its simplest form, spirituality can mean living a life based on choices and actions that make you feel more connected with your deepest values.

The *old* definition of happiness says that your satisfaction and contentment in life are based on what you *have*—things like wealth, achievements, possessions, and recognition by others. But unfortunately, when those things fade and disappear, so too will your happiness. The promise of *The New Happiness* is that there is a better way to experience satisfaction and contentment in life based on your spiritual values and actions; this is a happiness that lasts even when you come up against unavoidable obstacles and losses in life.

Spirituality Based on Psychological Principles

Built upon the research and principles of acceptance and commitment therapy (ACT)[vi]—namely, establishing values, developing mindfulness,[vii] and committing to acceptance—*The New Happiness* will lead you through a course of self-introspection and skills-building to help you develop your own set of spiritual principles. ACT is a successful, modern form of psychotherapy designed to help people in emotional and psychological pain. While this book draws

---

vi   The processes of ACT have been shown to strengthen and support spiritual growth (Hawkes et al., 2014; Dworsky et al., 2016; Santiago and Gall, 2016; Nieuwsma et al., 2015; Nieuwsma, Walser, and Hayes, 2016; Amin, Maroufi, and Sadeghi, 2017).

vii   Mindfulness and meditation have been shown across hundreds of empirical studies to significantly improve physical, psychological, and spiritual well-being (Murphy and Donovan, 1997; Baer, 2003; Walsh and Shapiro, 2006).

on those principles—as well as on key practices from a multitude of religions, faiths, and philosophies—it goes *beyond* what is usually discussed in the therapy room.

The focus here is not on treating depression, anxiety, and other forms of psychological problems (although that might happen naturally while working with this book). Instead, the focus is on improving the overall quality of your life and your sense of well-being. *The New Happiness* will help you shape your spirituality through your values-based actions, rather than helping you define your religious and philosophical beliefs. In short, *The New Happiness* defines spirituality as a process of "doing" rather than a process of "believing."

Doing Versus Believing

For some people, beliefs related to faith, religion, and spirituality can be confusing or even harmful. Maybe you were raised without spiritual beliefs of any kind and now you feel like something is lacking in your life. Or maybe you once held certain religious beliefs but now you question their validity. Or worse, maybe you were once the target of abuse in the name of religious beliefs, and as a result, you gave up believing in anything spiritual. If you fall into any of these categories, you're not alone. For thousands of years, scholars, theologians, and believers have argued and fought in favor of their own beliefs about God, spirituality, and religion. But rather than get bogged down in these debates, *The New Happiness* encourages you to engage in spiritual actions without arguing about who's right or telling you what you should believe. We're proposing that you can still feel spiritually fulfilled without knowing the answers to all of the spiritual questions. If you believe in God, that's okay, but if you don't believe in God, that's okay too.

The New Happiness is an action-based spiritual system—*not* a belief-centered spiritual system. It is designed to help you identify your spiritual values and live according to those values, in order to give your life a deeper sense of meaning. (Throughout this book we'll use "spiritual values" and "values" interchangeably to mean the same thing: the principles and standards that guide you toward a more rewarding and spiritual life.) In many ways, this book is a secular guide to spirituality and no previous belief system is required! We, the authors, are encouraging you to embody your spirituality and to allow it to inform everything you do, to affect all of your choices; to live your life according to your spiritual values and allow your behaviors to be an expression of your spirituality. This is the true "secret" to lasting happiness.

Why Choose The New Happiness?

If you're reading this book, it is likely that you fall into one or more of the following categories:

1. You want to be happy in your life and the thought of finding a "new" kind of happiness sounds hopeful.

2. You feel like something is missing in your life, and you suspect that seeking spirituality will fill the gap.

3. You're familiar with the principles of ACT—or you've been in ACT treatment—and you want to try something new and related.

4. You've been in other forms of psychological treatment, such as dialectical behavior therapy (DBT), and after finding success stabilizing your emotions, you aren't sure what to do next. You may be thinking, *Now what? Where do I go from here?*

In each of these cases, connecting with spirituality is your next step—identifying your values, your life purpose, and your actions during moments of choice, and finding out where true happiness comes from.

What to Expect

Throughout this workbook, you'll be led through various exercises. It's important that you follow the chapters in the order in which they appear, because each of the new skills builds on the skills learned in previous chapters. In total, the book is a gradual learning process, taking you from simple spiritual exercises in the beginning to more advanced skills in the latter chapters.

- First, we'll help you redefine what spirituality means, focusing on "what you do" rather than "what you believe."

- You'll learn a simple form of mindful meditation.

- You'll work on discovering your values and acting on those values during the moments of choice in your life, when you have to decide: "What should I do?"

- You'll learn another wisdom meditation to help you connect both with your own inner wisdom—to help you make wiser choices—and with something spiritual outside of yourself—whether that's your own sense of God, a higher power, or the universe—to feel connected and gain guidance.

- You'll learn about barriers to spirituality and how to overcome them.

- Finally, four of the last chapters of the book deal with advanced concepts of spirituality to help you develop even deeper connections with people and the things you value. You'll learn about compassion, making amends to others, the importance of accepting impermanence, and finding a personal state of grace—a lasting sense of happiness that is created through living a spiritual life.

As you begin learning the various skills in this book, you'll notice that many of them require you to find a few minutes of your day when you can sit still, in a quiet place, and breathe. We are not going to ask you to isolate yourself for several hours each day, but we do hope that in the beginning you can find at least three to five minutes. (Later in your practice you can spend more time as needed.) In addition, you might want to think about creating a special "spiritual" environment for your skills exercises. Maybe find a quiet room or a corner of your garden where you can put a comfortable chair or cushion to sit on, place some inspirational spiritual pictures or decorations in the space, and begin looking for a spiritual "talisman" to use in your exercises—an object that holds special spiritual significance for you.

In addition, it's important to understand that changing anything in your life requires a combination of work, motivation, and determination. Creating a spiritually fulfilling life for yourself is no different, but it's well worth your efforts. This book requires you to make changes in what you *do*, rather than just making changes in what you *think*. You're going to learn new actions to help you change old habits and learn how to make more fulfilling choices in your life. But don't be intimidated—the process is gradual, and you'll be rewarded along the way with a feeling of connection to other people, your own inner wisdom, and a greater sense of knowledge bigger than yourself.

Remember, your life is a creative process. Each day you get to choose how you will act, *regardless of your circumstances*. Each day you get to choose between doing "business as usual" and maybe finding happiness, *or* living according to your spiritual principles and being happy no matter what happens. We hope you'll choose to make your life a creative *spiritual* process and find new happiness for the rest of your life.

Chapter 1

Finding Spirit

We all carry spirit within us. Spirit is our own deepest self or immortal soul (depending on your own personal belief). It is our connection to all of conscious life. Spirituality is nothing more and nothing less than knowledge of spirit; knowledge of our purpose, our mission, and the truth about what matters and what doesn't in this life.

Living is making choices. We make hundreds of choices every day. A lot of these choices focus on pleasure, comfort, safety, and avoiding pain. Seeking pleasure and doing all that we can to stay away from pain have nothing to do with spirit. Those are concerns driven by our bodies and minds. Spirituality, on the other hand, is about making choices that are aligned with the deepest truth of who we are and why we're here.

Religious laws and canons are sometimes connected to spirit, and sometimes distorted by human needs and ambition. Religious theologies and cosmologies that tell us about God and heaven are sometimes informed by spirit, and sometimes are a fabrication of human hopes and fears. While religion often provides comfort and guidance, the most direct route to spirit is through the awareness held in your own deepest self or immortal soul. This book is about unlocking the knowledge that's already within you and learning to make choices based on your spiritual core.

Growing Spirituality

You can grow your knowledge of spirit and the relationship to your spiritual core through the use of special practices. Over the millennia, countless methods have been devised to access or strengthen spiritual awareness. These methods include:

- Rituals and ceremonies

- Prayer

- Drugs

- Compassion practices

- Sleep, food, or oxygen deprivation

- Lucid dream states

- Many forms of meditation

- Chanting

- Shamanic drumming

- Induced pain states

- Sacred songs and melodies

- Trance states

- Channeling

- Reading scripture

- Asceticism

- Stimulus deprivation, and many others.

Many of these practices create unreliable results, outcomes that vary according to the needs, fears, beliefs, expectations, and level of susceptibility of the practitioners. Certain practices may be helpful to Person A, discouraging for Person B, and send Person C completely into chaos. Practices that rely on altered states (deprivation, drugs, pain, and trance states) are especially problematic for spiritual growth because the physical and psychological reactions can be so mixed, and there is little research to support their effectiveness.

Practices you'll learn in this book are all based on mindfulness and meditation. They have been tested, by ourselves and others, and been found to increase spiritual awareness, improve emotional well-being, and develop values-consistent behavior. In other words, they help you bring your life choices into alignment with what really matters. Specifically, these spiritual growth practices can help you:

- Find clarity about your life's purpose and mission.

- Find deeper compassion for yourself and others.

- Learn to *act* on your values, your deepest truth and wisdom, at every moment of choice, even if that choice is sometimes hard or painful.

- Learn to *see* the moments of choice you face every day that can take your life and your relationships closer to or further away from what you most value, what you most care about.

- Learn to *hear* your own deepest truth and the wisdom that comes from spirit.

- Learn how to *face* and accept pain rather than letting it lead you away from what you value, away from your wisdom, away from the life you want to live.

The First Doorway to Spirit: Your Breath

For thousands of years, the breath has been used as a focus for meditation. This is no accident because breath is the *source*, the center of your physical life. The in and out of each breath, as it holds your attention, can do three important things that strengthen your spiritual awareness:

1. Breath-focused meditation quiets emotions. A large body of scientific research demonstrates the power of meditation to soften intense feelings so you become less emotionally driven and overwhelmed. Even meditating two to five minutes a day can make a difference, because you learn to *watch* your feelings instead of being carried away by them.

2. Breath-focused meditation allows you to observe and distance yourself from thoughts. Runaway thoughts, in the form of rumination and worry, play a major role in human distress, and they can occupy your mind to the point that spiritual awareness gets lost. Meditation teaches you to merely *watch* thoughts rather than get lost in them; to quiet your mind so you can listen to spirit.

3. Breath-focused meditation creates awareness of the moment of choice and strengthens your ability to choose wisely. The moment of choice occurs when negative thoughts and emotions gang up and start driving you to do something—anything—to get rid of the pain. Pain-driven actions are often damaging; over time they have a corrosive effect on our lives. Meditation can strengthen your ability to see the alternative, spiritually wise actions you could take instead.

The way you breathe is very important. The way we're going to suggest that you breathe, during the meditations in this book, might feel unnatural at first. But please be patient and don't judge yourself or give up. Most of us were never taught "how" to breathe. We just did it from birth. However, many of us have picked up some unhelpful habits that might be interfering with our ability to relax and focus. So, right now, as you're reading this, put one hand on your chest and one hand on your belly. Notice which hand moves more. Many people will notice the hand on their chests moving more and might even notice that their bodies tend to rock or sway as they breathe in and breathe out. This isn't "bad," but it's not the most efficient or effective way to breathe. Ideally, you should be breathing with the support of your *diaphragm*, the muscle at the bottom of your rib cage. When the diaphragm moves down toward your belly button it causes your lungs to fill with air. However, in order for it to move easily and properly, you have to release your abdominal muscles and allow them to expand, rather than holding them tight and rigid. (Look at the way an infant breathes for a good example—all the movement is in the belly, without any upper chest rocking.) This is called "diaphragmatic breathing." As you continue to place one hand on your chest and one hand on your belly, do your best to mentally shift the movement you feel to your abdominal area. As you slowly breathe in, allow your belly to gently inflate like a balloon, and as you slowly exhale, allow your belly to gently and effortlessly deflate. The key here is to take "slow" breaths, *not* "deep" breaths. You do *not* have to fill up your entire lung capacity when you breathe. Rather, allow yourself to find a slow steady rhythm that allows a natural amount of air in and out of your body. (If you breathe too deeply or too rapidly you might start to feel light-headed or tingling in your lips; this means you're hyper-ventilating. If so, stop the process, relax, recover, and then try again later using a slower, steadier rhythm. Try imagining an ocean wave slowly moving onto the shore and then slowly retreating and you'll probably find a slow, steady rhythm.) It might take some time to make this transition from upper chest breathing to diaphragmatic breathing, but don't give up, it's worth it. We the authors believe that slow diaphragmatic breathing is one of the most helpful skills you can learn in this whole book! It's not absolutely necessary to master diaphragmatic breathing before you begin Still Mind Meditation (see below), but a few minutes of practice before you start will be helpful.

Still Mind Meditation

The particular breath-focused meditation you'll learn now is called "Still Mind Meditation." This introductory practice is valuable because it's simple and easy to learn. Most importantly, it's versatile and can be used anytime, anywhere. Still Mind Meditation also forms a foundation for more advanced practices, such as the Compassion Meditation and Deep Knowledge Meditation you'll learn later.

Your Talisman

Still Mind Meditation is aided by having a *talisman*, an object of meditative focus. This could be something you look at, like a drawn symbol or photograph, or it could be a small, easily carried object that you touch while meditating. This talisman, whatever you choose, should represent peace, wisdom, the presence of God or spirit or higher power, love (of or for someone in particular, or universal love), nature, or spiritual awareness or spiritual truth of any kind.

Whether you choose to hold or look at your talisman, it will be a symbol that connects you to spirit. Examples that people have used include:

- A small drawn circle representing the divine or infinity.

- A tide-worn stone representing the eternal movement of the ocean.

- An acorn symbolizing life.

- A photo of someone beloved.

- A small piece of granite taken from a mountaintop.

- A photo of a sunrise.

- A symbol of love, such as a ring.

Still Mind Meditation Process

To begin, fix your eyes on the talisman or hold it in your hand. After a moment, begin to include awareness of your breath by noticing the movement of your diaphragm and your belly. Slowly breathe in and allow your belly to gently expand like a balloon. And then slowly exhale, allowing your belly to gently and effortlessly deflate. Now just note your breath by saying "in" to yourself on the in-breath and "out" on the out-breath. Thich Nhat Hanh, a famous Buddhist monk and peace activist, recommends this method. If you prefer, you can note your breath by counting each out-breath until you get to four breaths, and then start over. By noting the breath and observing the movement of your diaphragm, you are focusing attention on your center, your life force.

Inevitably, as you focus on the breath, thoughts will arise. These may be memories, worries or plans about the future, ruminations about the past or why things happen, or judgments about yourself and others. As soon as you notice a thought, return your attention to your breath. When you lose track of your breathing and your mind gets caught in a chain of thoughts, don't judge yourself or feel that you've failed. This will happen again and again. It's what our minds do. Just bring your attention back to your diaphragm, the in and out of your breath.

As you meditate, your thoughts are likely to slow down and seem less urgent. They won't stop, but they'll get further apart. There will be spaces in between that feel peaceful and quiet, a soothing emptiness. Also, as your mind quiets, emotions may soften and quiet as well.

Our negative thinking drives so many of our painful emotions. As you observe and let go of worry or judgment thoughts and return to the breath, you may also watch certain painful feelings diminish. Emotions don't last long (an average of seven minutes) unless they are reinforced by our disturbing thoughts, so Still Mind Meditation, practiced daily, can have a calming effect on your emotional life. You can literally learn to watch emotions—as you observe your thoughts—rise and crest and recede. The sequence is like this:

- Watch your breath.

- Notice and let go of each thought.

- Watch your breath.

- Notice your mind gradually get a little more still, and as a result,

- Your emotions, no longer driven by long chains of negative thoughts, feel softer and less overwhelming.

Practicing Still Mind Meditation

Still Mind Meditation should be practiced daily. Pick an event or situation that occurs each day (for example, morning coffee, resting in your big chair right after work, getting in bed) and tie Still Mind Meditation to it. Commit to yourself that you'll do at least two minutes of meditation at the appointed time.

It's important not to demand too much of yourself. At the beginning, do at least two minutes, but no more than five minutes, of Still Mind Meditation. Don't make this a big hill to climb; doing a little bit, regularly, can change your life. Later, after your routine is established, you can meditate longer—if you wish. But here's the rule: never expect to, or set a goal to, meditate for more than five minutes. If, in the middle of Still Mind Meditation, you want to go longer, that's fine. Extend the session. However, setting out to do longer meditations can discourage you and make you less likely to keep your daily practice. It's like going to the gym: if you plan a twenty- or thirty-minute workout, you'll probably go. If you plan a grueling "two hours or bust" circuit, you'll often start making excuses and skipping sessions.

Over time, you may want to increase your daily meditation sessions to two or more. That's fine. It can strengthen spiritual awareness and create more emotional benefits. But never demand more than five minutes of meditation at a time. We encourage you to start *today*.

Building Your Practice

- Spirit is your own deepest self or immortal soul, and your connection to all of conscious life.

- Spirituality is about making choices that are aligned with the deepest truth of who you are and why you're alive.

- The mindfulness and meditation practices in this book will help you increase your spiritual awareness, improve your emotional well-being, and develop your values-consistent behavior.

- Breath-focused meditation quiets emotions, allows you to observe and distance yourself from your thoughts, and creates awareness of the moment of choice while strengthening your ability to choose wisely.

- Practice breathing using slow diaphragmatic belly breaths, allowing your belly to slowly inflate as you inhale and slowly deflate as you exhale.

- Using Still Mind Meditation and your talisman, focus on your breath moving in and out of your body. If you notice thoughts arising in your awareness, do your best to return your focus to watching your breath rise and fall. Practice Still Mind Meditation two to five minutes a day.

Chapter 2

Your Values

What shapes our existence and determines the direction we'll take in our lives is our values. Our purpose, our way of navigating, is set by the core principles that guide us. Each decision we make, from how we speak to a misbehaving child to a choice of job or career, is influenced by our values.

Without values, each crossroad we reach in life has no signpost or markings, and our decision about which way to turn is based mostly on seeking pleasure and avoiding pain. But life is about more than pleasure and pain; it's about *doing* what matters and being the person—at each moment of choice—you want to be.

When your life feels like something is missing, when it feels wrong or without meaning, it's time to reconnect with your values and use them to make different choices. You've experienced pain in your life. You've had losses, hurts, and setbacks; there have been times when you've been sad, depressed, ashamed, or scared. And it's natural—in the face of pain—to make our lives about controlling, numbing, or somehow getting rid of the pain. But sometimes, when we are focused on getting rid of pain, our values—the things we care most about—can get lost.

Right now, as you are strengthening your spiritual awareness, it's time to reconnect to the things that matter to you. Identifying your core values will help you, in each moment of choice, to see and take the wise path. To get started, use the "Values Clarification Worksheet" that follows. Circle your top ten values on the list. As you do this, notice that values aren't goals. Goals are something you can accomplish and be done with—like getting a degree or buying a house. Values are directions, like always trying to learn, or having a safe and nurturing home. Values are a compass point, a heading, a guide toward all that matters to you.

Values Clarification Worksheet

Review the list below and circle your top ten values.

Accountability	Contentment	Efficiency	Grace
Accuracy	Continuous improvement	Elegance	Growth
Achievement		Empathy	Happiness
Adventure	Contribution	Enjoyment	Hard work
Altruism	Control	Enthusiasm	Health
Ambition	Cooperation	Equality	Helping
Assertiveness	Correctness	Excellence	Holiness
Authenticity	Courtesy	Excitement	Honesty
Balance	Creativity	Expertise	Honor
Belonging	Curiosity	Exploration	Humility
Boldness	Decisiveness	Expressiveness	Independence
Calmness	Dependability	Fairness	Ingenuity
Carefulness	Determination	Faith	Inner harmony
Challenge	Devoutness	Family	Inquisitiveness
Cheerfulness	Diligence	Fitness	Insightfulness
Clear-mindedness	Discipline	Fluency	Intelligence
Commitment	Discretion	Focus	Intuition
Community	Diversity	Freedom	Joy
Compassion	Dynamism	Friends	Justice
Competitiveness	Economy	Fun	Leadership
Consistency	Effectiveness	Generosity	Legacy

Love	Restraint	Success
Loyalty	Results-oriented	Support
Making a difference	Rigor	Teamwork
Mastery	Security	Temperance
Merit	Self-actualization	Thankfulness
Obedience	Self-control	Thoroughness
Openness	Self-reliance	Thoughtfulness
Order	Selflessness	Timeliness
Originality	Sensitivity	Tolerance
Patriotism	Serenity	Tradition
Piety	Service	Trustworthiness
Positivity	Shrewdness	Truth-seeking
Practicality	Simplicity	Understanding
Preparedness	Soundness	Uniqueness
Professionalism	Speed	Unity
Prudence	Spontaneity	Usefulness
Quality	Stability	Vision
Reliability	Strength	Vitality
Resourcefulness	Structure	Wellness

Now we're going to explore two very different kinds of values: *self-growth* and *service*. Self-growth values are focused on how you develop and take care of yourself as a person. Domains include things like creativity, health, education/learning, recreation, self-compassion, and personal self-care. Service values focus on your relationship to other people and the world at large; they are about giving to, caring for, and supporting things outside yourself. Domains include family, social relationships, community, nature and the environment, people in need, animals, and public policy.

On the two "Values Assessment Worksheets" that follow (*self-growth* and *service*), place a check mark next to the domains that are important to you, and write a key value that guides and influences your behavior. If you're having difficulty finding a value for a particular domain, go back to the "Values Clarification Worksheet" to get ideas.

Once you've identified a guiding value for each important domain, move to the right side of the "Values Assessment Worksheets." Here's the most important part: where you turn values into actions. Values by themselves won't make an impact on your life unless you act on them. An intention is something you're committed to doing—a specific action, at a particular time and place, that moves you in a valued direction. An intention is essentially a specific goal for enacting a particular value. Intentions aren't wishes or hopes; they are concrete plans, chosen behaviors that implement the values you care about. Make sure you've written down a values-based intention for every important domain. Your intentions will change over time as you accomplish some of them, and others will emerge. But at any point, your intentions are a blueprint for actions that will help you grow spiritually. (You can download a PDF of this worksheet at http://www.newharbinger.com/43379.)

Values Assessment—Self-Growth Values

DOMAINS	INTENTIONS/COMMITTED ACTION
Record your value under each important domain.	Record one specific thing you can do to turn your value into action. Include all the details. (When? Where? What? Who? etc.)
EXAMPLE *1. Personal Self-care and Health* ☑ Important to you? Key Value: *Wellness*	*I'm going to call this afternoon to make an appointment with my MD to get a long-overdue physical within the next 2 weeks. I'm also going to speak with my wife at dinner about going for a walk every night after we eat to help drop some of the extra weight I'm carrying around.*
1. Personal Self-care and Health ☐ Important to you? Key Value:	
2. Spirituality ☐ Important to you? Key Value:	
3. Creativity ☐ Important to you? Key Value:	

4. Leisure and Play ☐ Important to you? Key Value:	
5. Work and Career ☐ Important to you? Key Value:	
6. Personal Growth and Education ☐ Important to you? Key Value:	
7. Self-Kindness and Compassion ☐ Important to you? Key Value:	
8. Other: ☐ Important to you? Key Value:	

Values Assessment—Service Values

DOMAINS	INTENTIONS/COMMITTED ACTION
Record your value under each important domain.	Record one specific thing you can do to turn your value into action.
	Include the details. (When? Where? What? Who? etc.)
EXAMPLE 1. Family ☑ Important to you? Key Value: *Cooperation*	I'm going to speak with my wife tonight about dividing up the household chores so that I can help more and she will feel less overwhelmed.
1. Family ☐ Important to you? Key Value:	
2. Friendships and Social Relationships ☐ Important to you? Key Value:	
3. Community and Volunteerism ☐ Important to you? Key Value:	
4. Environment and Nature ☐ Important to you? Key Value:	

5. *People in Pain / Others Who Are Struggling* ☐ Important to you? Key Value:	
6. *Creative Expression* ☐ Important to you? Key Value:	
7. *Animals* ☐ Important to you? Key Value:	
8. *Politics and Public Policy* ☐ Important to you? Key Value:	
9. *Education and Teaching* ☐ Important to you? Key Value:	
10. *Other:* ☐ Important to you? Key Value:	

Values Compass

Every day you make choices that bring you closer or take you farther from your values. The way you move closer to values is to remember them. Right now, choose your two most crucial self-growth values/intentions and two most important service values/intentions. You're going to track each of these four intentions daily to see how close or far from them your choices take you. On the next page—the "Values Compass Assessment"—are four circles, each with a "V" at the top where you usually see north on a compass. "V," in this case, stands for Values.

Duplicate seven of these assessment pages—enough to fill them out daily for the next week. (You can download a PDF of the page at http://www.newharbinger.com/43379.) Write one of your four most important values/intentions above each compass. At the end of each day, you'll evaluate how close or far your actions took you from each intention by drawing a radial line from the center point of the compass to the outer edge. The closer you place the line to the "V" (north point of the compass), the more your actions were in alignment with your value/intention. A line pointing to the bottom (south) rim of the compass would mean your actions were the direct opposite of that particular value/intention. Observing how your behavior aligns with key life values is an important step toward spiritual growth.

Values Compass Assessment—Example

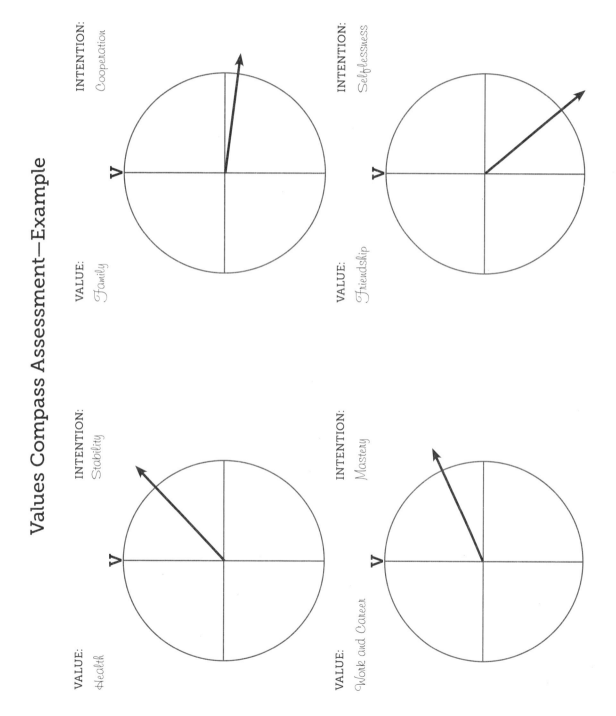

VALUE:
Health

INTENTION:
Stability

VALUE:
Family

INTENTION:
Cooperation

VALUE:
Work and Career

INTENTION:
Mastery

VALUE:
Friendship

INTENTION:
Selflessness

Values Compass Assessment

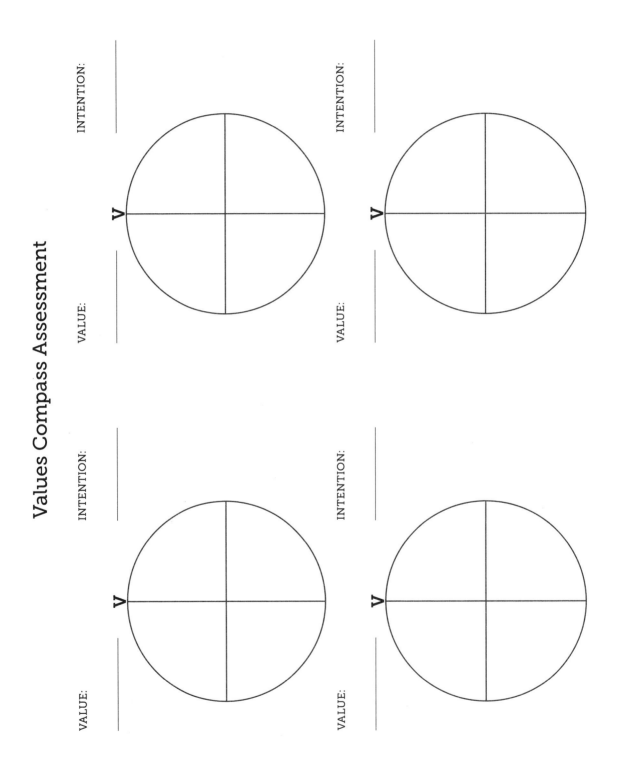

INTENTION:

VALUE:

INTENTION:

VALUE:

INTENTION:

VALUE:

INTENTION:

VALUE:

Your Highest Value

The next two exercises will help you identify your highest self-growth value and your most central service value.

Self-Growth Value: Trip to a Deserted Island Exercise

Go back to your self-growth values and review them all. Now imagine that you can have all of them in your life—without limits! Imagine that you're taking them with you on a trip to a deserted island, where you'll be for some time. You load your boat with your self-growth values and head out to sea. Before reading on, use the space below to create a ship's manifest—a list of the self-growth values that you packed on board. Put a star next to your highest value.

"Ship's Manifest" of Self-Growth Values

_____

_____

_____

_____

_____

_____

As you head toward the island, you notice that your boat is at risk of taking on water from the weight of everything you brought along. You'll need to toss one of your values overboard. Have a good look at your inventory. Which value would you toss away? Once you've decided, go ahead and cross it off your list.

Turns out that wasn't quite enough. You're still in danger of sinking. You'll have to pick another value to cast overboard. Which one will you choose now? Go ahead and select it, then cross it off your manifest. Your boat is lighter, but you're still taking on some water. It turns out you'll need to select another value to toss away. Go ahead and do that.

Continue with this exercise until you're down to one of your self-growth values. This will be the only value you can take with you if you're to make it to the island alive. Which one did you choose? And why did you choose it? Look to your heart and gut and see if there's something in that value that you feel strongly about. This one essential self-growth value is one of your passions. As you continue with your spiritual development, keep this key self-growth value at the forefront of your thoughts. It is likely that this value will govern much of your happiness, fulfillment, and sense of purpose in life.

(Exercise adapted from Strecher, 2016.)

Service Value: A Tug at Your Heart Exercise

Your pain can teach you something about what you care about. Think back over the years. Where have you suffered? Did the actions of other people contribute to that suffering? What was it that they did? Was the suffering connected to your own mistakes or ignorance?

Now see if you can imagine what you would need to restore your sense of wholeness, dignity, and justice.

Now expand your horizons to the world around you. Imagine seeing others going through pain and suffering similar to your own. You might imagine seeing this via television, movies, or other media, in your daily life, or in relationships with others who are important to you.

When you see others experiencing your suffering, how does that affect you? Does it tug at your heart? Do you feel a pull, a compulsion to act or defend, to reach out to alleviate that suffering, to right the wrongs or to create peace? This is important, so take some time with it.

Your pain will often point to your passions, and to where you feel most compelled to reach out to others in service.

(Exercise adapted from Strecher, 2016.)

Your two highest values can be lighthouse beacons for your spiritual life. Keep them in mind each day and do your best to observe any choices you can make that would impact these core values in a positive way.

Building Your Practice:

- What shapes your existence and determines the direction you'll take in your life is your values?

- Values are like compass points, they're headings that guide you toward all that matters to you; goals are actions that move you in the direction of your values.

- Self-growth values are focused on how you develop and take care of yourself as a person.

- Service values focus on your relationship to other people and the world at large; they are about giving to, caring for, and supporting things outside yourself.

- Use the "Values Assessment Worksheets" to identify key values in your life and specific actions you can take to fulfill those values.

- Use the "Values Compass Assessment" on a daily basis to determine if you're consistently taking actions that are in line with your values.

- Identify your highest self-growth value and your most central service value; these are the two values that will likely most influence your life and bring you the greatest sense of satisfaction in your life.

- Continue practicing Still Mind Meditation every day, for at least two minutes but for no more than five minutes.

- Start "checking in" with the way you're breathing throughout the day, even when you're not meditating, and do your best to use diaphragmatic breathing as much as possible.

Chapter 3

The Moment of Choice

The Still Mind Meditation you were introduced to in chapter 1 is about learning to focus awareness and to closely observe a single experience—breathing. If you've been doing Still Mind Meditation at least once a day, you are getting better and better at the skill of focused attention. This has many benefits, including slowing your mind and helping you feel more relaxed. But perhaps the greatest benefit is the ability to pay attention to the *moment of choice*.

Every day we make choices. The problem is that our choices are often made (1) without awareness that a choice is there, and (2) without using our wisdom and values. A practice, or discipline, is necessary to develop wise choices based on the core spiritual values you identified in chapter 2. It starts with the intention to recognize when choice is present. Here are the signs that a *moment of choice* is at hand:

1. When there's a strong emotion, it almost always means that a choice is present—to act on values or to act on emotion-driven urges. For example, sadness makes us want to withdraw, anger makes us want to attack, anxiety makes us want to avoid, and shame makes us want to hide or attack. But these emotion-fueled urges may not always align with core values of who we want to

be. Noticing that strong emotion brings not only urges but choices is an essential part of our spiritual growth.

2. When you are in pain—whether emotional, mental, or physical—it usually means a choice is present. Pain creates an urgency to do something to control, get rid of, numb, soothe, or in some way diminish the pain experience (more about this in chapter 4). The things we do to manage pain quite often diverge from our core spiritual values. Getting angry when frustrated, giving up in the face of disappointment, withdrawing or shutting down when something hurts physically, and drinking or drugging away unpleasant experiences may temporarily relieve distress, but they take us far from the path of who we want to be.

3. When you experience strong desires or impulses, it usually means a choice is present. Desire can be a motivator to seek positive experiences—or destructive ones. Sexual desire, for example, can begin a deep bond of love and partnership, but it can also fling us into relationships with people we don't like or are merely using. The desire for any pleasure—from eating a banana split to streaming videos to buying a new car—is often a moment of choice that can bring us closer to or further from values. All strong impulses, especially those that involve leaving (relationships, jobs, places, and so on), buying, attacking, or withdrawing, likely require a moment of choice to evaluate the impact on our values.

To summarize: These are the three states that we must train ourselves to observe: emotion, pain, and desire. We must learn to watch each because they are the moments in life where we're most likely to face spiritual choices. These moments, over time, define our lives and mark the path of our existence. In combination, they determine who we become and what we are about.

The Morning Intention

The Morning Intention is a way to prepare yourself to recognize moments of choice. Many people begin their day with a short ritual, prayer, or pledge to remind themselves of their purpose—the values they live by. Priests say their morning "office." Some doctors reread their Hippocratic Oath. Some peace officers remind themselves of their role to "serve and protect." Many parents who rise, tired and bleary-eyed, to dress and feed their children before work, recall that they do it for love.

You, too, can set an intention in the morning. Starting this week, you can begin each day with a commitment to observe one of these states (high emotion, pain, or desire) throughout the day. Tie the commitment to a particular event every morning. It might be your first cup of coffee, your shower, when you shave or put on your makeup, or while driving to work. That moment is your cue to remember: "Today I'm watching my [emotions, pain, or desires]. That's my job—to see the choice each time [emotions, pain, or desires] show up."

The Morning Intention, during the first week, rotates across the three states. That's because it's easier to notice one experience rather than three. After the first week, shift your intention to mindfully observing *all three states* during the day—high emotion whenever it shows up; pain whenever it occurs; and desire as it drives you toward impulsive behavior.

After the first week, form an intention to notice any of the three states *at the moment it occurs.* As soon as an emotion becomes recognizable, as soon as pain—in any form—shows up, as soon as desire or a strong impulse hits you, commit yourself to see it and be aware of the *moment of choice.*

Moment of Choice Journal

Now it's time to observe what happens as you face daily choices. Did you get caught up in attempts to manage pain and seek desire, or did you find a way to act on values? Observing the outcomes of each choice—without judgment or self-attack—is crucial to steering your life toward whatever truly matters to you. The process, everyday, of noticing and remembering the decisions you make is the foundation of spiritual growth. The "Moment of Choice Journal" that follows will help you record the outcomes of these decisions and strengthen your commitment to acting on values. The journal covers a single week; we suggest that you duplicate copies so you can record your moments of choice over a two- to three-month time span. (You can download a PDF of the journal pages at http://www.newharbinger.com/43379.)

Moment of Choice Journal

Monday

1. What did I observe (emotion, pain, or strong desires/impulses) and what were the details?

_____

_____

2. What choices showed up? _____

_____

3. What choice did I make? _____

_____

4. How did my choice align with my values? _____

_____

Tuesday

1. What did I observe (emotion, pain, or strong desires/impulses) and what were the details?

_____

_____

2. What choices showed up? _____

_____

3. What choice did I make? _____

_____

4. How did my choice align with my values? _____

_____

Wednesday

1. What did I observe (emotion, pain, or strong desires/impulses) and what were the details?

_____

_____

2. What choices showed up? _____

_____

3. What choice did I make? _____

_____

4. How did my choice align with my values? _____

_____

Thursday

1. What did I observe (emotion, pain, or strong desires/impulses) and what were the details?

_____

_____

2. What choices showed up? _____

_____

3. What choice did I make? _____

_____

4. How did my choice align with my values? _____

_____

Friday

1. What did I observe (emotion, pain, or strong desires/impulses) and what were the details?

_____

_____

2. What choices showed up? _____

_____

3. What choice did I make? _____

_____

4. How did my choice align with my values? _____

_____

Saturday

1. What did I observe (emotion, pain, or strong desires/impulses) and what were the details?

_____

_____

2. What choices showed up? _____

_____

3. What choice did I make? _____

_____

4. How did my choice align with my values? _____

_____

Sunday

1. What did I observe (emotion, pain, or strong desires/impulses) and what were the details?

_____

_____

2. What choices showed up? _____

_____

3. What choice did I make? _____

_____

4. How did my choice align with my values? _____

_____

Making Sense of Your Choices

In the beginning, most of your recorded choices will be focused on managing pain or seeking something pleasurable. That's okay. It's where we all start as we try to grow spiritually. Don't be discouraged, and don't give up keeping your journal. Things won't change if you don't pay attention to them. You can learn about yourself by observing how you respond to emotions, pain, and desire. And, over time, you can change those patterns of response because you become *conscious of choice as it happens.*

What do you tend to do when you're angry, sad, afraid? How do you respond when your body hurts? How do your desires and impulses overtake you, and what do you do when feeling desire intensely? The objective is not to judge, but to notice. Jiddu Krishnamurti, a twentieth-century philosopher and religious teacher, once said that the only road to change is to observe what you do—right now. Change depends on seeing what is. And when *what is* seems misaligned with *who you want to be,* evolving and changing is a natural outcome. So keep your journal, no matter what happens. Spiritual change will be inevitable.

Building Your Practice:

- Continue Still Mind Meditation once per day.

- Update your intentions on the "Values Assessment Worksheets" that you completed in chapter 2. Regularly review your intentions for both self-growth and service values. Remember that intentions often change as you accomplish goals and circumstances shift in each domain of your life. Ask yourself, "How can I put my values into action in new ways?" If a particular goal or intention has been realized, ask yourself, "What's next? How, specifically, can I move toward that value now?" Use copies of the "Values Assessment Worksheets" to write in an updated intention as outcomes and circumstances change.

- Begin each morning with your intention. For the first week, rotate through the three stages: high emotion, pain, and desire. Then make it your Morning Intention to observe all three during the day, and to notice the choices between your values and your old pain- and emotion-driven responses.

- Each day, note in your "Moment of Choice Journal" at least one choice you made. Try to observe and write about this choice with interest rather than judgment. Remember that observing, by itself, will bring about spiritual change.

Chapter 4

How Pain Shapes Our Spirituality

Earth is a hard place to live. There isn't a person on this planet who hasn't faced pain. You know from your own life how many things have the potential to distress you. Much of our pain is uncontrollable—it hits us and there isn't much we could have done about it. And often as not, there's not a lot we can do to stop it. Psychologists call it *uncontrollable pain* for just this reason. Examples of this kind of pain include:

- Loss. The most extreme case is loss through death, but we can lose relationships in many ways, including rejection. And the relationship is not always to a person—it can be loss of an animal, a place, a group or affiliation; loss of a job, of financial security; loss of wellness, of physical and mental abilities; loss of objects that have value or meaning; loss of time.

- Hurt. The sense of being judged and found wanting, of being wrong or bad or *less than* in someone else's eyes.

- Physical pain and disease.

- Fear. This includes the fear of death, loss, hurt, and physical pain.

- Uncertainty. This is our condition—not knowing when accidents, traumas, losses, failures, rejections, or illnesses may happen. And we live with a constant undernote of such vulnerability.

- Failures and mistakes. While in theory mistakes could be avoided, usually we are doing our best and making the best choices we can see at the time. Even if we're doing our best, most failures and mistakes *are* unavoidable. And the pain they bring can't be avoided either.

- Wounds from our family of origin. We have little control over how we were treated as children, or the level of dysfunction in our family. And we may have little control over how these old wounds have scarred us in the present. For example, negative beliefs (schemas) formed about ourselves and our relationships in childhood often cast a shadow over how we see ourselves now, and how we react to relationship stresses.

- Choices made by others. Pain caused by the choices of others is often well beyond our control. Other people have their own will, their own fears and needs, and their own perceptions—and their actions will usually be based on what they need and believe rather than what's good for us.

What Pain Is

Here is our situation on this planet: every day we are vulnerable to pain we can't control. This pain is not punishment, not some just desserts for sin or wrongdoing. This pain is not a sign of failure at life. It is just being human; it is just the necessary consequence of living on earth. When you can shed blame and judgment as you face moments of pain; when you realize that most pain is out of your control and no one's fault; when you focus on living your values rather than avoiding unavoidable distress, the *experience* of pain changes. It becomes something to face and learn from, an opportunity to act on what *truly* matters, rather than endlessly struggling to control and avoid.

Pain is an opportunity to *learn* and *choose* (values versus pain avoidance). That's why we encounter it—so we can continue to learn and to make better choices based on our spiritual values.

Pain Coping Strategies

Over the course of human history, we've developed a lot of coping strategies to deal with pain. They fall into three categories:

1. **Accept, allow, observe the pain.** Let it take its course, gradually evolving and morphing as you do your best to live your values. The pain and values-based actions live side by side.

2. **Problem-solve the pain.** Sometimes this works and the pain goes away. When it doesn't, it usually means the pain isn't in your control. Trouble is, you can't problem-solve most losses. Or hurts. Or fear and uncertainty, wounds from childhood, or choices made by others. *But you can act on values while feeling the pain.*

3. **Avoid the pain.** There are many, many forms of pain avoidance:

    *   Drink or drug the pain away.

    *   Substitute another emotion—like anger—to hide the pain.

    *   Distract yourself from the pain.

    *   Emotional numbing: trying not to feel or care about the pain.

    *   Cognitive avoidance: trying not to think about or remember the pain.

    *   Situational avoidance: staying away from situations that remind you of the pain, or that are associated with it.

    *   Withdraw, shut down.

    *   Attack what seems to be the source of the pain.

    *   Give up, stop trying in the face of pain.

How Do You Cope with Pain? Exercise

You'll find the "Coping with Pain Worksheet" on the next page. It will give you an opportunity to examine ways that you've dealt with distress, and the outcomes of each coping strategy.

In column 1, write a very brief description of a distressing experience under each category; this can be an example from the recent past or from further back. In column 2, write how you coped with the pain (you can put down more than one coping strategy). In column 3, write how, in the long run, your strategy worked. Did the pain get worse, better, or stay the same? Were there other positive or negative outcomes? (You can download a PDF of this worksheet at http://www.newharbinger.com/43379.)

The Coping with Pain Worksheet

Typical coping strategies: • Accepted/faced the pain • Acted on values • Used problem solving • Used alcohol/drugs • Substituted another emotion • Used distraction • Used emotional numbing • Tried not to think/remember • Avoided situations • Withdrew • Attacked • Gave up

CATEGORY	COPING STRATEGY	OUTCOMES
Example: Loss Girlfriend left me.	*Avoided the places we used to go together & the people we knew.*	*Started feeling even lonelier & didn't have much fun in life.*
CATEGORY	COPING STRATEGY	OUTCOMES
Loss:		
Rejection:		
Physical pain:		
Hurt:		
Fear:		
Uncertainty:		
Failure/mistake:		
Wounds from family:		
Choices made by others:		

Where Your Pain Leads You

As you examine your "Coping with Pain Worksheet," what do you notice? Is there a predominant way you cope? Do certain categories of pain lead you to cope in different ways? How often are you able to accept the pain and move toward things you value versus trying to avoid or suppress the pain?

How do your coping methods turn out? Do different ways of coping have different outcomes? Are you mostly able to control your pain and reduce its impact, or are your coping methods sometimes making things worse? Importantly, what happens when you try to avoid pain altogether—does this result in positive outcomes, or does the focus on pain avoidance get in the way of doing the things that matter to you?

In the journal entry space that follows, write the conclusions you've reached after considering the above questions.

Where My Pain Leads Me: Conclusions

_____

_____

_____

_____

_____

_____

In many ways, pain is the single factor that most influences us spiritually. When avoiding pain is our primary coping response, we often focus away from what matters (values) and single-mindedly pursue whatever provides pain relief. This way of responding to pain can get in the way of spiritual growth. You can see if this is true for you by looking at your conclusions above. If you tend to accept—rather than fight—uncontrollable pain, you may have more energy for acting on your spiritual values. Again, your own experience will tell you if this is true.

Pain and Spiritual Growth

As discussed above, pain leads to choices—moving toward spiritual values or keeping our lives focused on numbing and avoidance. But the uncontrollable pain of life also leads to opportunities for growth. It can light the way to important life lessons, provide a deeper sense of our life's purpose and mission, and offer greater clarity about what we most value. In fact, in the profession of psychology there is currently a whole field of study focusing on *post-traumatic growth*, that is, the positive personal development and even potential benefits that can result from experiencing pain and even severe trauma.

Please review again your "Coping with Pain Worksheet." Think about the distress you've documented there, as well as the related difficult experiences. In the journal entry spaces below, give thought to answering the following questions:

What's the most important lesson you've learned from a distressing life experience (write more than one if you want):

_____

_____

_____

_____

_____

What has your pain taught you about your core purpose in life?

_____

_____

_____

_____

_____

What spiritual value does your pain most elevate and make you recognize?

_____

_____

_____

_____

_____

How have you experienced any post-traumatic growth as a result of your pain and suffering?

_____

_____

_____

_____

_____

Building Your Practice:

- Continue Still Mind Meditation once per day.

- Update your values-based intentions so new intentions replace any that have been accomplished or discarded. If new values have emerged from your journaling about pain, add them to your values list.

- Continue your Morning Intentions. If you have rotated through the three states (high emotion, pain, and desire) twice, now include the intention to watch for all three throughout the day. In your intention, include the commitment to watch for the moment of choice when you can act on values or on old pain- and emotion-driven responses.

- Keep recording outcomes from these moments of choice in your "Moment of Choice Journal." Try to be nonjudgmental and accepting of whatever happens. This is a spiritual growth process that will take time.

Chapter 5

Deep Knowledge Meditation

By this point in your spiritual growth and development you've been practicing Still Mind Meditation, focusing on your self-growth and service values, and becoming more aware of (1) when you make choices and (2) which types of choices you make. (Hopefully those choices are ones based on the values you identified!) With practice, you've probably begun to notice some positive results, even if they're modest ones. Maybe you've recognized that when you do Still Mind Meditation your thoughts appear to slow down—at least a little bit—or that you feel more relaxed after you've completed the exercise. Or maybe you've noticed that your life feels a little bit more hopeful or filled with purpose, because you've been focusing on your values and incorporating them into your life more regularly. Maybe you've even gotten a glimpse into what your true *life purpose* might be—the task or value that would make you feel spiritually aligned and give your life true meaning. (We'll talk more about finding your life purpose in later chapters.)

Now, the next step in your spiritual development is to learn Deep Knowledge Meditation. Deep Knowledge Meditation will help you answer the questions you have about your life and clarify your choices before you make them. In essence, it's like hitting the "pause" button before you make a decision, looking for spiritual clarification, and then hitting "play" to actually make the decision. For some people who grew up with traditional spiritual practices, this might sound like "praying for an answer" or "asking God what to do." And if you're lucky enough to get answers to your prayers when you ask questions, then keep doing it. But if that's not part of your tradition—or if you feel like you never get answers to your prayers—then maybe you'd be willing to try something different. If you would like to access your own inner wisdom and intuitive truth, try using Deep Knowledge Meditation.

You can think of "deep knowledge" as being the sum of all the earthly wisdom that you've gained in your life plus the spiritual wisdom that is innate in all of us—spiritual wisdom that connects us with each other, the universe, and the divine. Often in life, we are taught to trust only our rational thoughts—the thoughts that are logical and supported by facts and research. But many of you might have already had the experience of knowing that something is "true" or "accurate" without knowing exactly why. This type of knowledge is called *intuition*. The practice of using Deep Knowledge Meditation balances your rational thoughts with your emotions, impulses, and natural spiritual intuition. Later, in chapter 8, you'll also explore using Deep Knowledge Meditation to connect with spiritual entities outside of yourself that may be meaningful to you, such as God, angels, and spirit guides. But for now, think of using Deep Knowledge Meditation as a tool to help you explore your own inner knowledge and spiritual wisdom.

Deep Knowledge Meditation Instructions

To begin, think of a problem you wish you had an answer for. For right now, the first time or two that you use Deep Knowledge Meditation, don't pick something that would radically affect your life, such as "Should I quit my job and move?" Rather, pick some more modest question, like "Should I join a gym?" (With more practice, you can later tackle the bigger questions about your life.) Write down this simple "yes or no" question. Now, find a comfortable place to relax where you won't be disturbed, and begin breathing as you did in the Still Mind Meditation. Also, use your talisman if it has helped you focus and relax. Next, imagine yourself connecting to the sense of "spiritual intuition" you carry inside yourself. Use your imagination. Perhaps you imagine a brilliant white light at the top of your head or maybe you imagine a glowing warmth in the center of your solar plexus. Whatever works best for you is okay, as long as it helps you feel a connection to your own inner wisdom, guidance, or spiritual intuition.

Then, after you've experienced a sense of calm, ask yourself the question that you wrote down and open yourself up to whatever you are shown in your imagination or given in some other way. Maybe you'll see an image depicting what you should do, or maybe you'll hear words. You might even just get a "sense of what to do." Do your best to receive the information without judging it. Just listen and be still. Try to be patient until you receive an answer.

Part of the process of performing Deep Knowledge Meditation is to balance your thoughts, feelings, and inner wisdom. If you become overwhelmed by painful emotions or judgmental thoughts during the process of asking your question and receiving an answer, just do your best to focus on your breathing, your talisman, or your connection to your intuition. Let the negative judgments float past like clouds in the sky without getting attached to them. Continue focusing on your breath and talisman as you connect with your intention to know what you should do.

Deep Knowledge Meditation is about choices, behavior, and doing. Visualize the situation or person that forms the source of your question. Notice what you see or hear in response to your question. Experience the desire to know what the "wise action" might be. Continue waiting with the intention to know until the wise action is seen or understood. Again, the answer may be in the form of words, a picture, or just a sense of knowing. The action you are to take might be expressed in many ways. You might be shown that you need to say something specific or you might be shown that you need to express something nonverbally. Leave yourself open to all possibilities. Wait until you know what the wise response is. Usually you can tell what the right thing to do is because it is accompanied by a sense of health, higher knowledge, or clarity.

When you get your answer, be appreciative. Your expression of gratitude will help open the channel and connection again in the future. This can be done by simply saying "Thank you," silently or aloud, or it could be something as formal as you want it to be. Next, write down whatever information you received. It's possible that your answer might be obvious, but it's also possible that your answer might not make much sense to you now but will in the future. Recording the answer is vital so that you can refer to it again at a later time. Write down as many of the details as you remember. Including what the experience as a whole was like.

Recording your answers is also important for another reason. In the beginning, it might seem like this act of asking questions to your higher self or spiritual intuition is nothing more than "talking to myself." However, if you start to record your answers, you're likely to see that they are accurate and in line with your values. You're also likely to see that the answers start to come more easily the more frequently you practice the meditation. In some ways, recording your answers is like gathering evidence to prove to yourself that the answers to your toughest questions are within your realm of knowledge and understanding.

Use the "Deep Knowledge Meditation Log" on the next page to record your question, review the meditation instructions, and record your answers for future reference. Make additional copies of the log for future use. (You can download a PDF of the log at http://www.newharbinger.com/43379.)

Deep Knowledge Meditation Log

Date: _____

Question: _____

_____

_____

- Find a comfortable place to relax where you won't be disturbed and begin breathing using Still Mind Meditation. Use your talisman if it has been helpful.

- Imagine yourself connecting to the sense of "spiritual intuition" you carry inside yourself. Use your imagination to see yourself connecting to it.

- Ask yourself the question that you wrote down.

- Express your desire to know what the "wise action" might be with regard to your question.

- Remain open to whatever answer you are shown in your imagination or given in some other way (for example, a vision, words, or a feeling).

- Be grateful for whatever you receive and do your best not to judge yourself or the response. Express your gratitude for receiving an answer.

- Record your answer for future reference.

Answer: _____

_____

_____

_____

_____

_____

_____

Example of Using Deep Knowledge Meditation

Alex had been using Still Mind Meditation for two weeks and had experienced some amount of relaxation in his body and peace in his mind as a result. So he decided to use Deep Knowledge Meditation to begin seeking answers about what to do with some of the "roadblocks" in his life. To begin, he did five minutes of Still Mind Meditation while sitting in his bedroom with the door locked, so his roommate wouldn't walk in on him. Then he focused on the talisman he held in his hand; it was a cross that his grandfather had given to him. Alex wasn't religious in a traditional sense, but the cross reminded him of his grandfather, who was now deceased, and it gave him a sense of being calm and relaxed. Next, Alex focused on his question. The lease was expiring on his apartment, and he was wondering if he should stay, and continue living with his roommate, or move somewhere else and live on his own. Alex continued his slow breathing, holding the cross in his hand, and focused on the possibility of moving. In his imagination, he saw a copy of his lease, his apartment, and then his roommate. He continued to breathe, holding his talisman, until he noticed that the pictures in his imagination started to change. Whereas before the image of his roommate was happy, his face now looked angry; the image of the apartment got darker; and suddenly the lease blew away in the breeze. Alex continued meditation for another few minutes, then opened his eyes, said thank you in appreciation for what he was shown, and then wrote his answers in the "Deep Knowledge Meditation Log." Upon reflection, Alex realized that he and his roommate had not been getting along for the last several months, and although they were good friends, Alex recognized that it was time to move on when the lease expired. He felt sad to be ending this chapter of his friendship, but he also realized that if he stayed roommates with his friend much longer, and they continued to argue, there was the possibility that their friendship might not last.

Regular Use of Deep Knowledge Meditation

Do your best to incorporate Deep Knowledge Meditation into your daily life. In the beginning, you're likely to have to sit still in a quiet place and practice Still Mind Meditation breathing techniques before transitioning into Deep Knowledge Meditation and asking your question. But with practice, you'll be able to simply pause, be still, take a deep breath, touch or remember your talisman, and seek a response to your question, whether you're at home or in the supermarket.

So, in addition to practicing Still Mind Meditation every day for five minutes or so, begin incorporating Deep Knowledge Meditation into your daily practice. If possible, start off each morning by recording a question about something you want answered. Then begin Still Mind Meditation and ask your question. Also, throughout the day, continue to focus on your self-growth and service values, and do your best to take action based on those values. In addition, continue to complete your "Moment of Choice Journal," so you can become more aware of the opportunities you have to make values-based decisions and actions.

Building Your Practice:

- Deep Knowledge Meditation will help you answer the questions you have about your life and clarify your choices before you make them.

- Begin with the Still Mind Meditation breathing technique.

- Imagine connecting to your inner wisdom or spiritual intuition.

- Be open to whatever answer you get, but wait for one that feels healthy, without being clouded by judgment.

- Use the "Deep Knowledge Meditation Log" to record your answers.

- Express your gratitude.

- Practice daily!

Chapter 6

Identifying Your Life Purpose

Hopefully you've had some positive experiences using the skills you've learned so far. You've been practicing mindfulness skills that can give you inner peace and clarity (Still Mind Meditation), as well as guidance (Deep Knowledge Meditation). You've also identified your core set of values (self-growth and service), and you've learned how to identify when there's a moment of choice in your life so that you can make decisions based on those values. Now it's time to take your spiritual development one step further—and it's a big step. In this chapter, we're going to explore how to identify your life purpose.

Why Your Life Purpose Is Important

Your life purpose answers the question of why you're here and what your life is about. This purpose is going to be the major theme in your life that influences most of your decisions and occupies most of your time. Your life purpose is going to be that special thing that people know you for when you're alive and remember you for after you're dead. Your purpose is like a chapter heading in a book: after you read the title, you know what's coming next. Similarly, once you define your life purpose, both you and others in your life will be able to predict the kinds of decisions you're going to make and the kind of person you're going to be, because—ideally—they will both be consistent and harmonious with your life purpose.

Many books have been written on the subject of helping you "discover" your life purpose. One best-selling book, *The Purpose Driven Life* (Warren, 2002), takes a particular religious perspective to help readers figure it out. If you share that religious belief and that book has been helpful, that's great! Or if you know your life purpose already, then you're even luckier. In those cases, this chapter can help you define it a little more. But if you're like many of us and have never thought much about your life purpose, then this chapter is going to be a truly eye-opening experience.

Throughout the ages, countless philosophers and theologians have debated the question: "What is the purpose of life?" Most of the answers have been complicated or were based on the teachings of whatever organized religion the person answering the question belonged to. The authors of this book don't belong to any organized religion, so for us the answer is much less complicated. The simple truth is this: *The purpose of your life is whatever you want it to be.* Whatever you spend the majority of your time doing and thinking about is the purpose of your life, because you are defining your purpose through those actions.

If I want the purpose of my life to be about taking care of others, then that's what I'll spend my time doing and the people in my life will recognize my purpose based on my actions. However, if I say that the purpose of my life is one thing but spend the majority of my time thinking and doing something different, then I'm not being honest with myself and others. In this case, my supposed life purpose and my actual life's *focus* might be completely different. My life's focus—where I put much of my time and energy—would be different from the life purpose that I defined.

The truth is, we all like to think highly of ourselves and to think that we're doing the "right" thing or a "good" thing. But if I said my life purpose was to create the deepest bonds of love possible with my children and my spouse, but I focused on spending eighty hours in the office and spending most of my time on the weekends catching up with work, then that statement wouldn't be accurate, would it? It especially wouldn't be true if my family relationships suffered or deteriorated as a result of all the time I spent at work. It might be more accurate to say that my life purpose was to "master my career" or to "create financial wealth for my family."

There are no "right" or "wrong" definitions for your life purpose, but it is important to recognize that your lifetime is limited. You will not live forever; there are only twenty-four hours in a day, and each second we're all getting a little older. No one knows when they'll die and your ability to do all the things you want is restricted by lots of other factors—like sleep, work, relationships, children, your health, and so on. So it's very unlikely that you will be able to put an unlimited amount of time and resources into all the areas of your life. You're going to have to make some choices and you're going to have to find a balance amongst your time, energy, resources, and relationships.

In this book, we share the belief that there is no predetermined purpose for your life. We do not believe that some deity has already planned that out for you. We believe that you get to choose your own life purpose and that you can change your life purpose at any time—your life purpose does not have to be the same for your entire life. Sometimes the circumstances of people's lives change dramatically—like when they get married or have children—and then their life purposes might change as well. But remember, choose your life purpose wisely and use your identified values for guidance, because whatever subject you identify as your life purpose is the same subject that will occupy much of your time, your actions, and your thoughts. If it's not a purpose that makes you feel fulfilled and satisfied, then much of your life is going to feel unfulfilled and unsatisfying as well.

Can Making Money Be My Purpose in Life?

If you want the purpose of your life to be "making money," then you'll find that you'll spend most of your time and energy focused on accumulating financial assets. As a result, other areas of your life might get neglected, like your relationships or your health. It's not that these areas of life are mutually exclusive, and it's not that money is "bad." However, spirituality is about your relationship with life and other living things, while money is only a tool to serve other purposes.

Spirituality is about connecting with other people, nature, the divine, and your true self—who you really are. So if you define your life purpose as connecting with (or accumulating) nonliving things—like money—then your connection with life and living things will likely be put on hold. Again, this isn't "good" or "bad," it just is. The purpose of your life is whatever you want it to be, but we encourage you to make it about connecting with others, the divine, spirit, and/or your higher self. These are the areas where you will find true fulfillment and satisfaction.

Choosing a Life Purpose to Connect with Others

So, does this mean that it's "wrong" or "bad" to choose a life purpose that benefits you too, or to choose a purpose that you find fun, interesting, or exciting? No, of course not. But we do encourage you to think about how that purpose can benefit others as well. For example, it would be perfectly fine to say, "My life purpose is to become a world-class photographer." But consider how much more spiritually fulfilling it might be to add, "My life purpose is to become a world-class photographer—so that I may bring joy to other people's lives." Or even, "My life purpose is to discover new insects in the rainforest of Brazil—so that others may learn and appreciate the diversity of life that exists there." In both of these examples, you would be taking your own personal interests and connecting spiritually with others.

Choose Your Own Life Purpose

Lastly, please remember that we're talking about *your* perspective on *your* life purpose, not somebody else's opinion about what you should do—like your parents', society's, or your spouse's.

Using the space below, list four or five of the major goals or purposes you've fulfilled (or tried to fulfill) in your lifetime so far. Do your best to just list them spontaneously, without thinking too critically. Just list the first ones that come to mind.

_____

_____

_____

_____

_____

_____

_____

Now look at the list you created and identify what goals and purposes came from you and what goals and purposes were imposed on you by other people. For example, were they your parents' goals or your goals? Then consider how happy or fulfilling your life has felt so far. Have you felt unsatisfied because you've been trying to fulfill someone else's goals? Or have you been unhappy because the life purpose you're living isn't the one you would have chosen for yourself?

What's really important is the answer to this question: "What do *you* want the purpose of your life to be?" Many people feel stifled or depressed for their entire lives because they've been fulfilling another person's definition of life purpose rather than their own. Don't make that same mistake. Figure out what's going to make you feel fulfilled, happy, and meaningful—using your own set of values—and make that the purpose of your life.

Do your best to use the following exercises to help you define your own life purpose.

Life Purpose Meditation

In many cultures, such as those of the Native Americans, it was common to go on a "spirit quest" to seek guidance about one's life purpose. The person who was looking for guidance might be led through an elaborate ritual or might spend days in a remote place hoping to make contact with a deity, a spirit guide, or a deceased ancestor. Often, the answer would come in the form of a sign or a feeling that would then have to be interpreted by someone more experienced with spirit quests. Similarly, in other cultures like that of the Tibetans, it was common to consult an oracle—a spiritual shaman—who would go into a trance in order to consult the spirit world for guidance on the person's behalf. Many more examples could be mentioned, but it's sufficient to say that human beings have been seeking guidance from the spiritual world for thousands of years, and the Life Purpose Meditation is just another similar tool.

The Life Purpose Meditation is a form of meditation and creative visualization that builds on the other meditations you've already been practicing, namely Still Mind Meditation and Deep Knowledge Meditation. As in Still Mind Meditation, you will need to use diaphragmatic breathing to help you calm your body and mind. And like Deep Knowledge Meditation, the Life Purpose Meditation encourages you to turn inward for guidance and to use the power of your imagination.

After calming your body and mind and turning your mental focus inward, leave yourself open to the possibility of connecting with your higher self, that spiritual part of you that stays connected to the divine even while you live your life on earth. While practicing this meditation, silently ask yourself the question, "What is the purpose of my life?" The answer, most likely, will not come immediately. You might need to wait several minutes, or you might even need to repeat this exercise several times over several days. This exercise will require you to be patient and to accept whatever information you receive without judgment or criticism. Remember, you might not get a clearly defined response to the question, "What is my life purpose?" You might see a symbol, or hear a sound, or just have a feeling. Whatever you receive, honor it and accept it without judgment. If the answer doesn't make sense to you right away, write it down and come back to it in the near future to determine if it makes more sense.

Read through the exercise below before beginning. If the instructions are too much for you to remember, try recording them on your smartphone so you can play them back and listen. Just remember to record them slowly, take long pauses, and allow yourself time to sit quietly and patiently. Also, if you're concerned about time, set an alarm for whatever free time you have.

Life Purpose Meditation Exercise

To begin, sit or lie down in a comfortable position in a quiet place where you won't be disturbed for the next fifteen to thirty minutes. Just as you've practiced, close your eyes and start using slow diaphragmatic breathing. If it helps, you can place one hand on your belly to remind yourself to release your abdominal muscles. As you slowly breathe in, allow your belly to gently inflate like a balloon, and as you slowly exhale allow your belly to gently and effortlessly deflate. The key here is to take *slow* breaths. Allow yourself to find a slow, steady rhythm that allows a natural amount of air in and out of your body. Continue breathing this way for a few minutes until you start to feel calm and focused. *(Pause for two minutes if recording.)*

Now, take another breath and imagine the air entering your heart, the center of your being. Notice the movement of your breath into your heart center. You might imagine your heart center to be a brilliantly glowing green or pink ball of energy and with each breath you are feeding your heart white healing light that connects you to all the goodness in the universe. Imagine your breath moving into that ball of energy. Bring your attention to that place. Allow every breath you take to deepen your connection to the center of your body, the source of your life. This is the place where you know what is most important, where you remember all the lessons you have learned. It is also the place where you can connect to your higher self and spirit.

Now, make a space in your heart, in that glowing ball of energy at your center. Imagine the space as a clearing in a lush forest. A meadow of grass and moss, in sun and shadow. This is the place for you to wait, to watch and to listen. Imagine yourself in this clearing and find a spot where you can rest and be still. It might be a hollow in the ground, or a stump, or even a rock to lean against. As you wait there, silently ask yourself, "What is my life purpose? What is it that I'm meant to do for the highest good of all?"

Now, settle into the place you've chosen and listen to whatever you hear. Watch for whatever catches your eye, even if it's just a branch moving in the wind or the grass rustling. In time, if you listen and watch long enough, something will show up in the clearing. It may come through the trees, or out of the sky, or it may just appear. Don't force it or try to make something happen. Just wait for it as long as it takes.

Whatever visits you is safe and means only the best for you. Whenever it comes, it will bring a message. Something you've been waiting to know about your purpose, what you came here to do in this life. You may recognize whatever comes as a symbol, or it may just carry the message to you as a sudden knowing, or as a feeling or an awareness.

You have only to wait in the clearing. There's no need to force it. Just allow yourself to wait and see what arises. Let time pass and be patient. Continue to breathe slowly and steadily. But stay alert, because the visit could come at any time.

After you've been given your answer, or some information, express your gratitude to your higher self or the divine. Then take several slow breaths, and whenever you feel ready, open your eyes and return your focus to wherever you are.

Life Purpose Meditation Journal

Use the journal on the next page to record whatever information you were shown or given. Again, remember not to judge, but rather to accept with gratitude. If your answer was clear, you might not need further guidance. However, if your answer was ambiguous—or if you didn't receive any information—you might need to repeat the exercise several more times, accumulating more information each time until your answer is clearer. Make additional photocopies of the journal if necessary.

And please remember, the Life Purpose Meditation is just one tool to help you clarify the purpose of your life. If it worked for you, that's great. But if it did not, please don't get discouraged, there are more exercises in this chapter to help you. (You can download a PDF of this journal page at http://www.newharbinger.com/43379.)

Life Purpose Meditation Journal

Date: _____

What information did you see/hear/feel? _____

_____

What does your answer mean to you? _____

_____

_____

Date: _____

What information did you see/hear/feel? _____

_____

What does your answer mean to you? _____

_____

_____

Date: _____

What information did you see/hear/feel? _____

_____

What does your answer mean to you? _____

_____

_____

The Tombstone Exercise

As was mentioned at the beginning of this chapter, our lifetimes are limited and no one can predict the moment that he or she will die. So ask yourself this: "If I died today, for what accomplishments or attributes would I be remembered?" Then, after you've answered the question, think about whether you like the answer. Because however you answered that question will probably say a lot about your current life purpose.

Your life will be remembered for the actions you took and the values you held—even if you never consciously defined your life purpose. For example, if I worked in a shoe store selling shoes my whole life, and then went home at night to a lonely apartment and avoided contact with other people, when I died that's what others would remember about me, that I was a loner who was good at selling shoes. It wouldn't matter much that I secretly dreamed of becoming a medical researcher to cure cancer, because I never actually worked toward such a goal and never defined my life purpose that way.

The Tombstone Exercise is an extremely important activity to help you imagine what others will remember about you after you've died. Granted, this exercise might be very painful for some people to complete, because they don't like to think about death and they certainly don't want to think about their own death. However, the truth is, we are all going to die, and the only thing you can do is try your hardest to make your life a spiritually fulfilling one. This exercise is critical to helping you see your current life more clearly and making any necessary changes. The purpose of the exercise is to help you put your current life into perspective. For example, are you living according to your values, or will the people who know you remember you for something different after you're gone? Similarly, are there actions you have taken for which you need to make amends, so that you're not remembered solely for your mistakes? (Chapter 11 will help you make amends.) Or are there actions that you still need to take, for which you want others to remember you?

Most of us are remembered for only two or maybe three generations at most after we've died, and then all memories of us simply fade away. (If you don't believe this, pause from reading this and write down how much you know about your deceased great-grandparents, such as what kinds of things they liked to do, who their friends were, and the exact location of where they're buried. Our guess is that you don't know that much about them, or even anything at all.) The Buddhists say, "All things are impermanent," meaning all things die, fade away, and are forgotten. You and I are no different. (Chapter 12 will discuss impermanence in more detail.) This exercise is not meant to be morbid, nor is it meant to insinuate that your life is pointless or purposeless; rather it is to remind you that we have a limited amount of time to do the activities we value and spend time with the people we love.

Exercise Instructions

As you prepare to complete the epitaph on your tombstone, think about two things: (1) "If it were written today what would it say about me?" and (2) "What would I prefer it said instead?" Complete both "Today's Tombstone" and "Tomorrow's Tombstone" on the following pages. Be honest, but not overly critical or judgmental. If you need to relax or still your mind before completing the exercise, sit quietly and use the Still Mind Meditation technique to calm your thoughts and emotions. Then use Deep Knowledge Meditation to seek clarity in your question about how you are going to be remembered.

After you've completed the exercise on both tombstones, notice the differences—if there are any. If there aren't any differences, you're on your way to completing a fulfilling life based on your values! However, for most of us, there are going to be differences between the life we're leading now and the life we would like to create based on our spiritual goals and values. Use the "Tombstone Review Worksheet" to highlight what changes you need to make and then do your best to identify the first steps that you need to take.

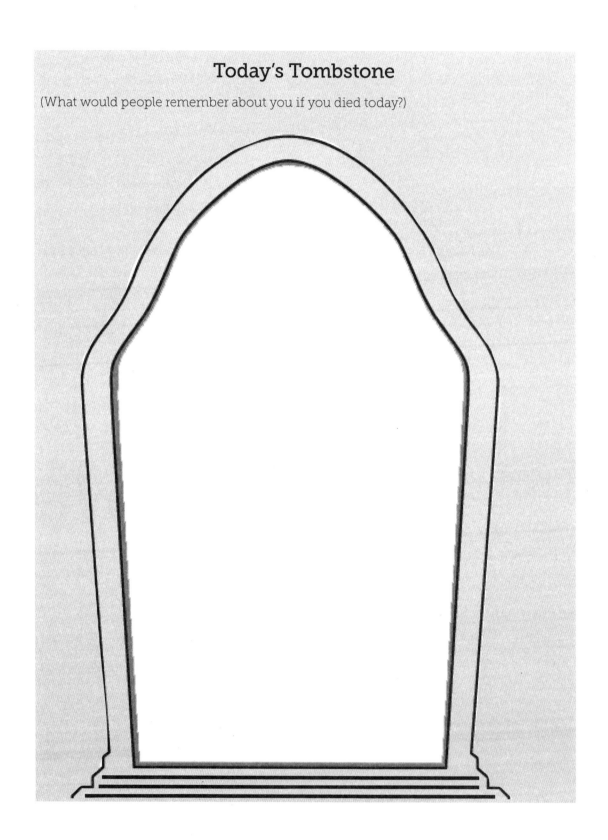

Today's Tombstone

(What would people remember about you if you died today?)

Tomorrow's Tombstone

(What would you *prefer* people to remember about you after you're gone?)

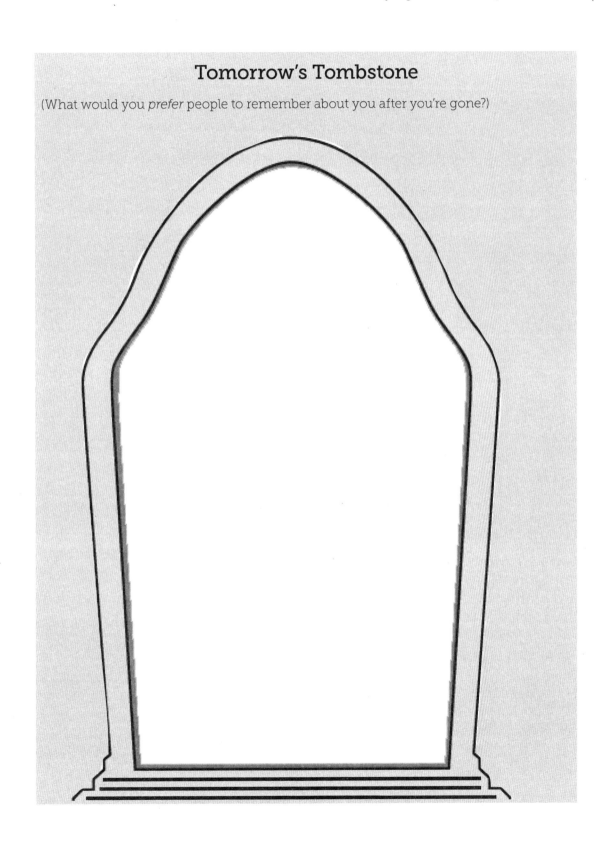

Tombstone Review Worksheet

1) What is the major difference between the epitaphs on the two tombstones?

_____

_____

_____

_____

_____

2) What are the values that are influencing "Today's Tombstone"?

_____

_____

_____

_____

_____

3) What is the life purpose expressed on "Today's Tombstone"?

_____

_____

_____

_____

_____

4) What are the values influencing "Tomorrow's Tombstone"?

_____

_____

_____

_____

_____

5) What is the life purpose expressed on "Tomorrow's Tombstone"?

_____

_____

_____

_____

_____

6) What is the first step you can take to move toward your new life purpose?

_____

_____

_____

_____

_____

_____

Create a Mission Statement for Your Life

Companies often create mission statements to quickly and easily remind their employees, investors, and customers of their purpose in the marketplace. For example, Google's mission statement is: "To organize the world's information and make it universally accessible and useful." The mission statement of Facebook is: "To give people the power to share and make the world more open and connected." Corporate mission statements are brief, easy-to-remember proclamations that motivate people when they face challenges and remind people about the company's purpose. Similarly, you need a mission statement for your life!

Creating a mission statement for yourself is a great way to summarize your life purpose. It's also a quick and easy reminder about the type of life you want to create when you're presented with a decision to make. Based on your experiences completing the two previous exercises in this chapter—the "Life Purpose Meditation" and the "Tombstone Exercise"—you were hopefully able to identify some core values and central ideals that are important to you. Write these down on the "Mission Statement Worksheet" below.

In addition, using the insight technique from Deep Knowledge Meditation, make an honest inventory on the "Mission Statement Worksheet" of your talents, abilities, interests, and pleasures; the types of friendships you have; and the moments of engagement, purpose, and happiness that you experience. Now ask yourself, what do all of these things have in common? What do these experiences and interests point to in terms of what you are here on this planet to be and do? Or, to think of it another way, if you were writing a book or a movie with a character like you, what would that character's life purpose be?

Now, put it all together and sum it all up in a mission statement for your life. Keep it simple, direct, and brief, maybe two or three sentences at most; make it something that's easy to remember. Keep it aligned with your values. It may be too complicated to convey all of your values, so maybe pick the most important two. For example, "I am a creative person who strives to discover spiritual experiences in his own life so that I might help others discover their own spiritual connections."

If you're having trouble summarizing your overall life purpose, instead focus on fulfilling a single value that you hold dear. Pick a value that you can commit to working on for the near future. For example, if you're having trouble but recognize that you want to be the best friend possible to those around you, maybe your mission statement would say something like, "I am a person who values friendships and family members, and who tries very hard to be a good friend to the people I care about. I will focus on helping others when I can, being a good listener, and spending my free time with others."

Hopefully it's clear why writing a "Life Mission Statement" is so important. Simply put, your statement has the potential to affect every choice that you make in your life, from the food you eat to how you choose to spend your free time. For example, if you value your friends and family and want to live a long life with them, then you'll hopefully also choose to eat healthily, exercise, and take care of yourself mentally and physically.

Mission Statement Worksheet

1. What are the core values or central ideals that play an important role in your life?

_____

_____

_____

2. What are your talents and special abilities? _____

_____

_____

3. What are your interests and pleasures? _____

_____

_____

4. What types of relationships do you have? _____

_____

_____

5. What are the moments in your life that make you feel the most engaged, purposeful, and happy?

_____

_____

_____

6. Is there anything else about you that influences your life purpose?

_____

_____

_____

7. Do these characteristics share anything in common that point to anything unique or special about you?

_____

_____

_____

8. Now combine all of these elements as best you can and write a mission statement for your life purpose. Keep it brief and to the point (two or three sentences at most). Let it be exciting and motivating. You'll know you hit the mark if you feel inspired after you read it.

_____

_____

_____

_____

9. How might your mission statement affect your future decisions and change the way you live your life?

_____

_____

_____

_____

10. When in the near future might you have opportunities to use your mission statement?

_____

_____

_____

_____

Building Your Practice:

- Your life purpose is the major theme in your life that influences most of your decisions and occupies most of your time.

- The purpose of your life is whatever you want it to be, and it can change over time.

- Using your identified values, make your life purpose about connecting with others, the divine, spirit, and/or your higher self.

- Use the Life Purpose Meditation to turn inward for guidance.

- Use the Tombstone Exercise to get perspective on your life and to help determine any changes that need to be made.

- Create a mission statement to summarize your life purpose; keep it simple, easy to remember, and brief—maybe two or three sentences at most.

- Also, continue to (1) establish your Morning Intention and observe instances of high emotion, pain, and desire throughout the day; (2) use Still Mind Meditation and Deep Knowledge Meditation to help you answer questions and clarify your choices; and (3) continue to use your "Moment of Choice Journal" to record outcomes and identify those moments.

Chapter 7

Preparing for the Moment of Choice

By this point on your spiritual path, you've clarified why spirituality is important to you, you've identified some of your values to help you make better decisions in your life, and you've been practicing Still Mind Meditation and Deep Knowledge Meditation to clear your mind and help you make better decisions. Hopefully, you've also identified your purpose in life. Now we'd like to highlight and strengthen another skill you're already familiar with from chapter 3. We'd like to prepare you further for those moments of choice in your life when you can act on your values, fulfill your life purpose, and create a more spiritually rewarding life for yourself.

Hopefully you've continued to fill in your "Moment of Choice Journal" from chapter 3, but let's review what you learned already. You can usually identify when there is an important moment of choice in your life—an opportunity to make a values-based decision—when you notice: (1) you're having strong emotions, (2) you're in emotional, mental, or physical pain, or (3) you're experiencing a strong desire or impulse. Strong emotions often make us want to avoid, attack, or withdraw—and not make values-based decisions. Pain creates an urgency to do something to control, get rid of, numb, soothe, or in some way diminish the pain experience. Again, this strategy often does not include acting on your values. And acting on strong desires or impulses often includes thoughtless or even reckless actions that may or may not move you into alignment with your values.

Returning to a discussion about the moment of choice is imperative, because changing anything in your life requires you to do something differently. And doing something differently includes recognizing what the old action was, identifying what the new action is, and then implementing that new action when the time is right. However, it's this last step that is always the hardest. For example, we all know that we should eat healthier foods. But when presented with the choice between eating a candy bar or a piece of broccoli, many of us are going to pick the candy bar, even though we know it's the less healthy choice. Maybe you think to yourself, *I really should choose the broccoli*, but then eat the candy bar anyway. Why does this happen, even when we know eating the broccoli is the *right* thing to do and we have already previously decided that it's what we *should* do? Again, there are many possible reasons:

- Maybe you're so emotionally aroused that the moment of choice goes unnoticed.

- Maybe you're in pain, and you choose to use a pain avoidance strategy—a quick fix to "feel better"—and the moment of choice gets forgotten.

- Maybe you're impaired—from drugs, alcohol, or medication—and you simply don't recognize the moment of choice.

- Maybe you're in an overbearing, controlling relationship—or a codependent relationship—and you abandon your values-based choices in favor of the other person's choices.

- Maybe you forget your values and intentions simply because you don't think about them often enough and so when the moment of choice arrives you don't know what to do.

- Maybe you miss your moment of choice because you're not in the present moment; instead, you're lost in your thoughts about the past or the future, and you don't even notice that a moment of choice is occurring right now.

- Or maybe you're simply not prepared to make a values-based decision; maybe you haven't spent much time using the "Moment of Choice Journal" and you haven't made any Morning Intentions, so you're just not ready.

So whether you've been making values-based decisions since reading chapter 3 or have been completely avoiding making values-based decisions for one of the above reasons, this is a chance to deepen your awareness of the moment of choice.

Planning for the Moment of Choice

To further prepare you to make values-based decisions, we first need to identify and review what happens for you when you are confronted with a moment of choice. The process that follows is going to require your imagination and honesty—about what you were thinking, feeling, and doing during the moment of choice.

Reviewing a Missed Moment of Choice

In order to review a missed moment of choice, and better prepare yourself for similar events in the future, you're going to need to use your imagination to recall a recent missed opportunity during a moment of choice. To begin, find a time and place where you can be alone and won't be disturbed for the next thirty minutes. Then, use Still Mind Meditation for two to three minutes to help you relax, center, and focus. Next, start to recall all of the elements of the situation you were in when the moment of choice was missed:

- Where were you?

- Why were you there?

- What time of day was it?

- What did the place you were in (or at) look like?

- Who were you with?

Keep imagining the details until you can recognize or remember how you started to feel emotionally in that situation, prior to the missed moment of choice. Maybe you can name the emotion (for example, "I was scared") or maybe you just remember that you had a physical sensation, like a tightness in your stomach.

Then, as the details and emotions of the event become more vivid, identify how you knew that you had a moment of choice in that situation. Were you overcome with strong emotions? Were you experiencing physical or emotional pain? Or did you have a strong desire to do something else? In addition, ask yourself what the choice was that you needed to make.

Next, do your best to remember what you did instead of making a values-based decision. Did you avoid something? Did you become paralyzed with fear or uncertainty? Did you give in to an impulse? Did you try to please someone else instead of acting on your values?

On the next page, you'll find the "Missed Moment of Choice Worksheet." Use the worksheet to review an important moment of choice in your own life that you recently missed.(You can download a PDF of this worksheet at http://www.newharbinger. com/43379.)

Missed Moment of Choice Worksheet

1. Identify a recent situation when you missed an important moment of choice:

_____

_____

2. Use Still Mind Meditation to relax and focus before recalling the details.

3. Recall the elements of the situation:

- Where were you? _____

- Why were you there? _____

- What time of day was it? _____

- What did the place look like? _____

- Who were you with? _____

4. How did the situation make you feel emotionally? _____

_____

5. How do you know you had a moment of choice? (Strong emotions? Pain? Impulse?)

_____

_____

_____

6. What did you do instead of making a values-based decision? (Avoid? Give in to an impulse? Become paralyzed? Please someone else?)

_____

_____

Example of a Missed Moment of Choice

Jane had been following the steps in this book, but still experienced difficulty when it came time to make values-based decisions during her moments of choice. She had been practicing Still Mind Meditation and Deep Knowledge Meditation every day. She had identified several self-growth and service values that were important to her. And she had identified her life purpose, namely, "To care for my customers as best I can, using my skills in business marketing; and to find interesting and creative ways to nurture my relationships with my family and friends in order to build stronger bonds with the people I love." Jane did her best to recognize some of the choices that showed up and to make values-based choices when she could, but she realized she was missing many opportunities and she didn't know why. Jane knew she needed more help.

Using the instructions in this chapter, Jane identified a recent situation in which there was another missed moment of choice. Jane had received a phone call a few days earlier, from her friend Sonya, with whom Jane hadn't spoken in a month. Jane saw Sonya's name on her phone's caller ID and she got nervous, so she let it go to voicemail. The last time Jane had heard from Sonya, Sonya had wanted to go to dinner and Jane blew her off. Now Jane suspected that Sonya was calling her back to tell Jane what a terrible friend she was.

Overall, Jane had two problems that often interfered with her choice making: (1) she struggled with anxiety, and (2) she worried about the future so much that she often wasn't fully aware of what was happening in the present moment. Because of her anxiety, she often avoided making any decisions at all. Obviously, Jane needed help and a plan in order to prepare for her next moment of choice.

Jane's example of reviewing her missed moment of choice is on the next page.

Jane's Example of a Missed Moment of Choice Worksheet

1. Identify a recent situation when you missed an important moment of choice.

Sonya called and I didn't pick up the phone.

2. Use Still Mind Meditation to relax and focus before recalling the details.

3. Recall the elements of the situation:

- Where were you? I was at work.

- Why were you there? I was working on a new project.

- What time of day was it? It was in the afternoon, during lunch.

- What did the place look like? The break room, it was busy, lots of people.

- Who were you with? I was sitting with my coworker, Don.

4. How did the situation make you feel emotionally? Scared, had a knot in my stomach.

5. How do you know you had a moment of choice? (Strong emotions? Pain? Impulse?)

I panicked when I saw her name on caller ID. I started to feel overwhelmed with a fear of rejection.

6. What did you do instead of making a values-based decision? (Avoid? Give in to an impulse? Become paralyzed? Please someone else?)

Instead of answering the phone I let it go to voicemail. Then I didn't even listen to her message. So I avoided...a lot. I still haven't listened to her voicemail. I felt paralyzed.

Rehearsing Values-Based Actions

Now we're going to move past detecting the moment of choice and identify the values-based actions that you wish you could make. First, you'll need to identify your values-based intentions for the scenario, and then you'll visualize and mentally rehearse the new values-based actions.

You're going to be preparing yourself for two different situations. You'll imagine yourself using the values-based actions in the original scenario—the original missed moment of choice. Then, you'll imagine yourself using values-based actions in future scenarios. Review the instructions below to identify the values-based actions that you intend to use in these scenarios. Afterward, we'll show you how to use those actions in both situations.

Instructions for Identifying Your Values-Based Actions

In order to identify your values-based actions—which you will use during a moment of choice—you're going to need to use your imagination again.

First, find a time and place where you can be alone and won't be disturbed for the next ten minutes. Use Still Mind Meditation for two to three minutes to help you relax, center, and focus.

Then, review your values from chapter 2 and identify which ones apply to the moment of choice for which you're rehearsing—either the original missed moment of choice or a future scenario. Also identify your life purpose from chapter 6 and see if that applies to the action you want to take—it's likely that it will.

Close your eyes and imagine yourself in the situation when the moment of choice arises—like you did in the last exercise—and again start to notice what you're drawn to do naturally. What are your old habits and old actions pushing you to do? Are they pushing you to avoid or run away? Ask yourself what will happen if you give in to those old actions.

Review your values and life purpose again and ask yourself, "What's the benefit of doing something differently this time? What are the benefits of acting on my values and life purpose?" In essence, "What's the payoff for behaving in a new way and doing something differently?" From a psychological perspective, actions that are rewarded get repeated, and those actions that don't get rewarded will be extinguished and disappear. So ask yourself what the benefit and reward will be from acting on your values rather than giving in to your old habits. Maybe it's an emotional reward, like "I'll feel more fulfilled," or

"I'll feel happier about my life." Or maybe the reward will involve others, like "My relationship with my wife will improve and feel more loving."

Identify the new, values-based action that will fulfill the intentions of your values and life purpose. Close your eyes and imagine yourself completing that action. Imagine yourself pushing through your natural desire to fall back on your old habits, and instead see yourself successfully enacting your value.

Finally, identify what the outcomes of your values-based actions are likely to be and ask yourself if those outcomes meet the intentions of your values, or if you need to modify your actions to fully meet those intentions. If you do need to modify your actions, pick a new action and repeat the process of imagining yourself doing it and identify the outcome again. If the outcome of your actions satisfies your values and life purpose, stick to it and use it.

On the following page is a "Rehearsing Values-Based Actions Worksheet" that will help you identify your values-based actions, your old actions, and the outcome of using your new actions. You'll use this same worksheet both to correct your original missed moment of choice and to prepare for future moments of choice. (You can download a PDF of this worksheet at http://www.newharbinger.com/43379.)

Rehearsing Values-Based Actions Worksheet

1. Identify your situation and the moment of choice for which you are preparing:

_____

_____

2. Find a safe environment to be alone and use Still Mind Meditation to relax and focus before recalling the details.

3. Review your list of values from chapter 2 and identify the ones that pertain to this situation:

_____

_____

4. Review your life purpose from chapter 6 and identify which part of it (if any) pertains to this situation:

_____

_____

5. Close your eyes and imagine yourself in the situation up to the moment when you need to make a decision about which actions to take.

6. What are you drawn to do naturally? What are your old habits? (For example, avoid or run away):

_____

_____

_____

7. What are the consequences of your old habits? _____

_____

_____

8. What are the rewards and benefits from acting on your values and life purpose? (For example, a pleasant emotion or a sense of connection):

_____

_____

9. What new actions can you take to fulfill the intentions of your values and life purpose?

_____

_____

10. Close your eyes and imagine completing the new actions and imagine the likely outcome.

11. Identify the likely outcome of your new action: _____

_____

_____

_____

12. Does the outcome satisfy the intentions of your values and life purpose? If yes, identify when you will complete this action. If no, return to step 9.

_____

_____

_____

Rehearsing Values-Based Actions for the Original Missed Moment of Choice

Now that you've identified the actions to fulfill your values and life purpose, we want to help you correct that original missed moment of choice. Obviously, we cannot go backward in time to do it. But you can do it in your imagination. By correcting the original missed moment of choice in your imagination, you better prepare yourself for similar events in the future, and, in a way, trick your brain into thinking that you *did* succeed in that moment by using your values-based actions rather than avoiding them. This is called *covert rehearsal.* In the world of sports psychology, this technique is frequently used to help top athletes correct the mental mistakes they made in previous games and better prepare for future games.

Using the instructions in this chapter for reviewing a missed moment of choice, take a few minutes to again recall that original scenario in which you failed to act on your values. Use your "Missed Moment of Choice Worksheet" from that scenario to help you recall all of the details. Then once again, close your eyes, use Still Mind Meditation to help you relax and focus, and then imagine yourself back in that same original scene. However, this time, when you're at the moment of choice, imagine yourself using your values-based actions. Recognize how hard it is to act on your values, but see yourself doing it anyway. Notice how your natural inclination might be to avoid, but again, imagine yourself doing it anyway. Identify the outcomes of your actions, both positive and negative, both for yourself and others. Ideally, rehearse this corrected version of the original missed moment of choice two or three times, or until it becomes easy for you to imagine yourself engaging in your values-based action.

Example of Rehearsing Values-Based Actions for the Original Missed Moment of Choice

Let's return to Jane's example. Remember, Jane had received a phone call a few days earlier from her friend Sonya, with whom Jane hadn't spoken in a month. Jane saw Sonya's name on her phone's caller ID and she got nervous, so she let it go to voicemail. The last time Jane heard from Sonya, Sonya had wanted to go to dinner and Jane blew her off. Now Jane suspected that Sonya was calling her back to tell Jane what a terrible friend she was, so Jane didn't answer Sonya's call.

So how was Jane able to use covert rehearsal to correct the original missed moment of choice in her imagination? First, she used Still Mind Meditation for a few minutes to help her relax and focus. Then she had to remind herself what her values were. In chapter 2, one of the service values that she identified was maintaining loving connections with friends and family, and when she completed her life purpose exercises in chapter 6, she stated that part of her purpose was to build stronger, more caring bonds with the people she loves.

Next, Jane imagined herself answering Sonya's phone call, even though she just wanted to avoid the whole situation and felt very anxious, even in her imagination! However, Jane played through the whole scene in her imagination and did her best to follow through on her values-based actions. Jane apologized to Sonya in the scenario, and even though Sonya was a little irritated, she forgave Jane and told her that she still wanted to be friends with Jane and make plans for the near future. Jane felt relieved and happy, and imagined herself hanging up the phone with a smile on her face.

On the following page is Jane's example of rehearsing values-based actions for the original missed moment of choice.

Jane's Example of Rehearsing Values-Based Actions Worksheet—For the Original Missed Moment of Choice

1. Identify the situation and moment of choice for which you are preparing:

Sonya called me at work and I have to answer her call and apologize.

2. Find a safe environment to be alone and use Still Mind Meditation to relax and focus before recalling the details.

3. Review your list of values from chapter 2 and identify the ones that pertain to this situation:

Maintaining loving connections with my friends and family.

4. Review your life purpose from chapter 6 and identify which part of it (if any) pertains to this situation:

To build stronger, more caring bonds with people I love.

5. Close your eyes and imagine yourself in the situation up to the moment when you need to make a decision about which actions to take.

6. What are you drawn to do naturally? What are your old habits? (For example, avoid or run away):

Avoid answering the call. Let it go to voicemail.

7. What are the consequences of your old habits?

Potentially, my relationship with Sonya might deteriorate, especially if I continue to avoid her.

8. What are the rewards and benefits from acting on your values and life purpose? (For example, a pleasant emotion or a sense of connection):

Creating a healthier, stronger relationship with my dear friend.

9. What new actions can you take to fulfill the intentions of your values and life purpose?

I need to answer the phone call and apologize to Sonya for avoiding her for so long.

10. Close your eyes and imagine completing the new actions and imagine the likely outcome.

11. Identify the likely outcome of your new action.

Sonya will be irritated but she will forgive me and want to make plans with me in the future.

12. Does the outcome satisfy the intentions of your values and life purpose? If yes, identify when you will complete this action. If no, return to step 9.

Yes, my actions will fulfill the intentions of my values and life purpose.

Rehearsing Values-Based Actions for Future Events

Just as covert rehearsal can trick your brain into thinking that you succeeded in the past, rehearsing values-based actions for future events is equally powerful to help you succeed. The goal here is to imagine future scenarios in which your old habits (such as anxiety or avoidance) are likely to get triggered and cause you to avoid using your values-based actions. But instead of avoiding, you're going to imagine yourself successfully using your new actions.

You might start this exercise by thinking of future events similar to your original missed moment of choice. Make a list of these events, and then start rehearsing the use of your values-based actions in several of them, or all of them. The more you rehearse these actions—even in your imagination—the easier they will be to perform in real life, when they occur. If any of these future events are within your control to initiate—like asking your boss for a raise, for example—rehearse the scene in your imagination until you feel comfortable and confident, and then initiate the scenario in real life. Again, use the "Rehearsing Values-Based Actions Worksheet" to help you identify your old habits and your new targeted actions.

Example of Rehearsing Values-Based Actions for Future Events

Let's return to Jane. She used covert rehearsal to imagine herself successfully answering Sonya's phone call. But then she realized that she still needed to actually return Sonya's call in real life and apologize. So how did Jane rehearse her values-based actions for the future? Essentially, she used the same steps she did in covert rehearsal, but this time she applied them to a future event that she intended to initiate in real life. First, she reminded herself what her values were. (Again, one of her service values was maintaining loving connections with friends and family, and part of her life purpose was to build stronger, more caring bonds with the people she loves.) Then Jane imagined herself preparing to call Sonya on the phone and noticed that she just wanted to avoid the whole situation again. Her anxiety and fear about what Sonya would say returned. However, she also realized that if she didn't call Sonya, their relationship would deteriorate, and Jane didn't want that to happen. She knew that the reward and benefit of calling Sonya was going to be a stronger relationship with her friend. The new action that Jane realized she had to take was to pick up the phone and call her friend, despite feeling uncomfortable while she was doing it. So she imagined herself successfully completing the action and imagined Sonya being initially irritated, but finally grateful that she had called. Then, after rehearsing this scenario three or four times, Jane finally got up the courage to call Sonya in real life, and it played out just the way she had imagined it. She was grateful to restore the relationship with her friend.

On the next page, review Jane's example of using the "Rehearsing Values-Based Actions Worksheet for Future Events."

Jane's Example of Rehearsing Values-Based Actions Worksheet—For Future Events

1. Identify the situation and moment of choice for which you are preparing:

Sonya called and I haven't called her back yet.

2. Find a safe environment to be alone and use Still Mind Meditation to relax and focus before recalling the details.

3. Review your list of values from chapter 2 and identify the ones that pertain to this situation:

Maintaining loving connections with my friends and family.

4. Review your life purpose from chapter 6 and identify which part of it (if any) pertains to this situation:

To build stronger, more caring bonds with people I love.

5. Close your eyes and imagine yourself in the situation up to the moment when you need to make a decision about which actions to take.

6. What are you drawn to do naturally? What are your old habits? (For example, avoid or run away):

Avoid making the call. Not call Sonya back.

7. What are the consequences of your old habits?

Potentially, my relationship with Sonya might deteriorate, especially if I continue to avoid her.

8. What are the rewards and benefits from acting on your values and life purpose? (For example, a pleasant emotion or a sense of connection):

Creating a healthier, stronger relationship with my dear friend.

9. What new actions can you take to fulfill the intentions of your values and life purpose?

I need to make the phone call even if I want to avoid it and even if it makes me feel uncomfortable.

10. Close your eyes and imagine completing the new actions and imagine the likely outcome.

11. Identify the likely outcome of your new action.

Sonya will be pleased and happy that I called her back and she will likely understand why I was avoiding her for so long. She's known me a long time and gets me.

12. Does the outcome satisfy the intentions of your values and life purpose? If yes, state when you will complete this action. If no, return to step 9.

Yes, my actions will fulfill the intentions of my values and life purpose. I'm going to call her this afternoon.

Creating a More Fulfilling Life for Yourself

Every person who has ever picked up a self-help book has the same goals: to improve his or her life and to feel happier. You too deserve a more fulfilling and happier life for yourself, and it all starts with making some basic changes to the actions you take. Ideally, after you've identified your values and life purpose, you would then start making healthier, more fulfilling choices in your daily life in order to stay true to your values and life purpose. But unfortunately, we don't live in an ideal world, and sometimes we need to practice and rehearse making healthier, more fulfilling choices based on our values so that those choices then become easier in the future. If you find this difficult, or if you get discouraged, please don't give up; just do your best and keep trying.

The next time you get discouraged, remember this story about the great American inventor Thomas Alva Edison. Mr. Edison was once asked by a reporter if he ever got discouraged because he had failed 1000 times before he finally invented the modern-day light bulb. Supposedly, Mr. Edison said something like, "I didn't fail, I just found 999 ways how not to make a light bulb."

Similarly, don't get discouraged if you don't make every decision based on your values. The more you practice, and the more you are aware of your decision-making opportunities, the easier it will become.

Building Your Practice:

- Preparing for the moment of choice will help you make values-based decisions and help you create a more spiritually fulfilling life.

- Changing any habit requires that you identify what the old action is, rehearse the new healthier action, and then implement that new action when the moment of choice presents itself.

- Use the "Missed Moment of Choice Worksheet" to help you identify how you knew a moment of choice was present and what you did instead of making a values-based decision.

- Then, use the "Rehearsing Values-Based Actions Worksheet" to identify what values and life purpose you want to fulfill in the moment of choice and what the personal payoff or reward will be for acting in a new, healthier way.

- Use covert rehearsal to imagine yourself successfully using values-based actions in your original missed moment of choice.

- Use future rehearsal to imagine yourself successfully using values-based actions in upcoming events when your old avoidance strategies are likely to get triggered again.

- Also, continue to (1) establish your Morning Intention and observe instances of high emotion, pain, and desire throughout the day; (2) use Still Mind Meditation and Deep Knowledge Meditation to help you answer questions and clarify your choices; and (3) continue to use your "Moment of Choice Journal" to record outcomes and identify those moments.

Chapter 8

Gaining Wisdom from Spirit

In chapter 5, you were introduced to Deep Knowledge Meditation as a means of relaxing, focusing, and looking inside of yourself for answers to important questions. This form of Deep Knowledge Meditation that you learned previously utilized your own inner wisdom and intuitive truth to gain insight before taking "wise action."

However, now we're going to discuss Deep Knowledge Meditation as a practice for connecting with something outside of yourself. This practice is much like using Deep Knowledge Meditation in the traditional sense of prayer. Essentially, you are directing your thoughts and questions to the other side of the plane of existence, beyond this world in which we live. Using Deep Knowledge Meditation in this way, you can direct your thoughts and questions to your concept of God, the collective consciousness of the universe, your relatives who have died and crossed over to the other side, spirit guides, angels, or even to your "higher self."

In this way, you do not need to rely solely on the limited knowledge and wisdom that you have learned and collected on earth over the years. You can instead reach beyond yourself for knowledge, wisdom, and answers by focusing on the spiritual realm beyond your earthly existence. To begin, think about the type of information you're looking for, and then ask yourself "who" or "what" might give you the best answer from the spiritual realm. And, as you'll see in the examples that follow, it's okay if you call on different entities for different types of questions. But again, be specific in your heart, thoughts, and words about what you're looking for and from whom or what you are seeking guidance. Think of the process as analogous to sending off a "spiritual email." You wouldn't leave the mailing address blank in your email and still expect to get a response. You'd have to pick a person to send it to. The same rule applies here, too. Being specific about your "spiritual addressee" makes it easier to get an answer to your question.

Also, be aware that the answers you get might not come in the clearest, most direct way, nor might they be understandable when you initially receive them. That's okay. Just do your best to express gratitude to whomever you asked for guidance, record your answer, and be patient. Sometimes the answer you receive will become clearer in the days or weeks after your meditation. Yes, unfortunately, the answers you are seeking will not always appear to you instantaneously, the moment you ask them. We know this is disappointing—for us too! However, we do not pretend to know exactly how the spiritual world works, nor exactly how our guides, higher powers, or higher selves communicate with us. Sometimes your answer might come as words, but sometimes it might also come as a feeling, or even a sense of knowing. There are many ways that your question could be answered. Do your best to remain open to all of them.

Also, the answers you get might sound foreign or surprising to you. Or the answers you get might be general in principle rather than specific advice or a specific set of instructions about what to do. For example, you might just feel a sense of love, but maybe that sense of love also gives you the confidence to make your own decision. However unfamiliar or unspecific your answer might be, do your best to remain optimistic that the answer will provide you some guidance.

Also, don't push away an answer that you don't like. It often happens that a person will ask a question of the spirit world and get an answer that he or she resists, because it runs contrary to what the person was secretly hoping to hear. But remember, the purpose of the spirit realm is to provide a sense of truth and guidance, not to affirm what you want to hear. Getting something different from what you expected might be hard to accept, but maybe that's the answer you needed to receive. Always do your best not to judge the answer you get. Simply express gratitude to whomever you sought guidance from and record your answer for later reflection using the "Deep Knowledge Meditation Log" at the end of this chapter.

Belief Versus Nonbelief

Hopefully, you will have noticed by this point in the book that we have not told you what you should believe from a spiritual theological perspective. We think that for each of us, it is a personal preference to believe in one God, many gods, or even not to believe in any god at all. Some of you might believe in angels, spirit guides, the souls of deceased loved ones who have crossed over, the goddess of Nature, or even space aliens. Some of you might call yourselves Christians, while others might identify yourselves as Jewish, agnostic, Hindu, Buddhist, atheist, Wiccan, or maybe have no label at all. We the authors certainly have our own spiritual beliefs, but we do not think that it is necessary for you to share our beliefs in order to use Deep Knowledge Meditation. However, we do hope that you believe in something beyond your earthly existence, something that you can connect to on some higher level during this exercise to seek guidance and clarification, even if it's just connecting with the universe-at-large.

For some people, this type of meditation is going to sound strange and feel even stranger. It may be hard for those people to believe that there are sources of wisdom on the other side of the plane of existence who care about them and communicate with them. And for others, it might be even harder to believe that there is another plane of existence at all! That's okay too. We encourage you to be skeptical. Do not accept our word that what we're suggesting is true—but maybe try it anyway!

And for those of you who think and feel like this might be a little too crazy to believe in at all, then we encourage you to think of this as just another form of meditation, in which you're using your creative visualization to connect with even deeper sources of your own wisdom. In any case, we hope you'll give it a try and see the results for yourself.

Deep Knowledge Meditation Instructions

To begin this advanced version of Deep Knowledge Meditation, first think of a question that you would like to have answered. When you were first introduced to Deep Knowledge Meditation in chapter 5, you were advised to keep your questions focused on smaller, practical issues until you gained more experience using the technique. Hopefully, by now you've been using Deep Knowledge Meditation to seek guidance on a regular basis and are more comfortable seeking clarification for larger, more complicated issues.

So first, think of a question, problem, or area of concern for which you would like some guidance or clarification. If you can't think of an issue off the top of your head, go back and review a list of your values or read through your mission statement again; maybe a thought will come to mind about something that requires clarification. For this example, write your question here:

_____

_____

_____

Next, think of the entity or source to whom you would like to address your question. Again, you might find that you send different types of questions to different addressees. For example, on questions of love you might think about your deceased Aunt Mildred, who had a wonderful marriage, while for questions about your career you send them to your spirit guide for advice. With whatever or whomever you feel connected, do your best to be specific about your question. For example, it might be too vague to ask "Should I consider moving and relocating my family?" Rather, consider something more specific, like "Should I relocate my family to Denver?" For this initial example, write the name of the person or source from whom you are seeking answers:

_____

_____

After you have clarified your question and identified your spiritual source of guidance, begin the meditation process using the instructions that follow. If you prefer to keep using the talisman that you chose in the earlier version of this meditation, then continue to use it to help you focus. If you prefer, use your smartphone to record the following instructions so you can listen to them.

First, find a place where you won't be disturbed for at least fifteen minutes. Turn off the ringer on your smartphone. Find a comfortable position to relax; whether you're sitting or lying down. Then use Still Mind Meditation to help you breathe and focus for three to five minutes. Allow your belly to gently expand as you breathe in and effortlessly collapse as you breathe out. Find a slow, natural rhythm of breathing and allow your body and mind to relax. *(If you are recording these instructions, pause here for three to five minutes while you continue to run the recorder, then resume reading aloud the instructions.)*

Now, begin to focus on the spiritual entity from whom you're seeking clarity. Do your best to hold this spiritual source in your heart and mind with a feeling of love and respect. If you have a visual image for this being, recall that image in your imagination as well. Do your best to use all of your senses to help you feel connected to your spiritual source. Is there a sound or voice that reminds you of your spiritual source? Then do your best to imagine it. Use your other senses of taste, touch, and smell to help connect you as well.

But most importantly, do your best to connect with the emotions of love and respect that you have for your spiritual source. Your emotional connections of love and respect are what will open the conduit of information flowing between you and your spiritual source of guidance.

Then, when you can feel that emotional connection, ask your question in your imagination or out loud and wait for a response. *(Pause here for two minutes if you are recording the instructions.)* Again, remember that your answer may not come in the form of words or even a clear set of instructions. Your answer may be a mental image that you see, an emotional feeling, a song, or even a physical sensation in your body. If your answer doesn't come right away, just do your best to remain calm, continue to focus on the rising and falling of your breath, continue to focus on that feeling of love and respect you have for your spiritual source of guidance, and keep repeating your question. *(Pause here again if you are recording the instructions.)*

After you receive your answer, in whatever form it comes, express your thanks and gratitude. Then take a few additional slow breaths and whenever you feel ready, open your eyes. *(End recording.)* Write your answer for this example on the space below and consider the action steps you might need to take next:

_____

_____

_____

_____

_____

_____

In the majority of cases, when you perform Deep Knowledge Meditation, some form of answer will come. Hopefully, it will be a clear message, an emotional feeling, or a general sense of knowing. Whatever you get, write it in the space above, and in the future use the "Deep Knowledge Meditation Log," on a following page. (You can download a PDF of the log at http://www.newharbinger.com/43379.)

What If You Don't Receive a Clear Answer to Your Question?

If your answer seemed vague, confusing, or even nonsensical, just do your best to respect the information you received and still record it. Remain grateful to whatever source you asked. Sometimes the answer you get will make more sense in the near future. Or perhaps you'll need to repeat the session of Deep Knowledge Meditation in another day or two to seek more clarification.

On the other hand, if no answer comes at all, that's okay too. It's disappointing for sure, but sometimes that happens—just like an email getting lost in cyberspace for some unknown reason. If you received no response at all—not a word, not a feeling, and not an emotion—then perhaps you should consider rephrasing your question, or even "addressing" it to another source of spiritual guidance, and then trying again.

Deep Knowledge Meditation Log

Date: _____

Question: _____

_____

Answer: _____

_____

_____

Action: _____

_____

_____

Date: _____

Question: _____

_____

Answer: _____

_____

_____

Action: _____

_____

_____

Examples of Using Deep Knowledge Meditation

Andrea was looking for guidance with her love life. She was currently in a relationship, but after four years, her boyfriend Bryan still did not express any interest in getting married or having children, and Andrea was considering leaving him. Andrea had always believed in nature spirits and had studied and appreciated aspects of the Wiccan religion. So when it came time to use Deep Knowledge Meditation, she decided to address her concerns to the all-wise Crone, one aspect of the Goddess acknowledged in Wicca. Specifically, her question was: "Should I end the relationship with Bryan so that I can possibly meet someone else?" Andrea started her meditation with some slow breathing to help her relax. Then she began focusing on an image of the Crone that she had seen in a book and began focusing on the emotion of love and respect she felt for the Crone and the Goddess as a whole. Then she asked her question. After a few minutes, she began to feel sad, and in her imagination she saw an image of herself walking out of the home in which she was raised. Looking back, she saw Bryan waving goodbye. Then, looking down the street, she had the sense that there was someone on the corner waiting for her, although she couldn't see the person clearly. Andrea felt like she had gotten her answer to end the relationship with Bryan, and felt reassured that someone else would be waiting for her when she did. Before stopping her meditation, she offered thanks to the Crone and to the Goddess for providing her guidance, and then recorded her answer in the "Deep Knowledge Meditation Log."

Mike had questions about his career. He worked in a retail store and had recently been offered a raise and a new position. However, the new position would require him to change stores and add an extra forty-five minutes to his commute each way. He wasn't sure what to do. Mike was raised in an Irish Catholic home, and although he went through all the religious rites and initiations as a child, he had fallen away from the church as an adult. However, he still felt an affinity for the Virgin Mary. There was something about the statues and the paintings of her that made him feel peaceful and connected to God, even though he no longer considered himself a member of the church. Mike began Deep Knowledge Meditation by focusing on his favorite image of the Virgin Mary, on his sense of love and respect for her, and on the question: "Should I accept the new position at work?" After several minutes of meditation and repeating the question, Mike saw several tall, beautiful redwood trees in his imagination. He didn't know what significance the trees had, and he started to feel frustrated. He was hoping to get a clearer answer. But even after several minutes more, nothing else appeared in his imagination. So Mike offered thanks to the Virgin Mary, ended the meditation, and recorded the trees in his "Deep Knowledge Meditation Log." For several more days, Mike continued to feel frustrated about what to do, and even got angry that the Deep Knowledge Meditation hadn't worked. But the time was quickly approaching when his supervisors expected him to make a decision. He decided that the best he could do would be to drive past the potential new location one last time and hope that he would be inspired with the right decision. Upon arriving at the location, he noticed a small grove of redwoods directly behind the store, which seemed unique. There were no other redwoods in that area. Mike smiled and felt relieved. There was his answer. He once again offered thanks to the Virgin Mary and emailed his supervisor to tell her that he accepted the new job.

Tim considered himself a "man of science" who wasn't raised with any religious beliefs and who didn't believe in god. However, he sometimes had the sense that there was more to existence than just life on earth, like maybe there was something else out there—whether it was something spiritual or maybe even extraterrestrial life. In general, Tim felt depressed and didn't know what to do about it. He had tried a few medications that his doctor had prescribed, but they didn't seem to make a difference. And he had tried talking with a counselor a few times, but that didn't help either. Tim began to wonder if he was missing something spiritual in his life, even though he wasn't sure what it might be. He decided to try Deep Knowledge Meditation by asking the general question, "What am I missing in my life?" and he decided to ask the question of the universe-at-large. In his imagination, he saw an image of a quasar star spinning in the middle of space, and he focused on a feeling of love and awe that he had for the universe and all of its celestial creations. After breathing, relaxing, and focusing, he did his best to stay connected with his visualization, and then he asked his question. Suddenly he saw himself in his imagination floating amongst the stars. He felt sad but wasn't sure why. Then, as he continued to feel himself "floating" amongst the stars, he began to feel a sense of peace and his body suddenly relaxed. He wasn't sure what to make of the peaceful sensation, but he just accepted it for what it was. When he was finished, he gave thanks to the universe, and wrote down his results in the "Deep Knowledge Meditation Log." For the next several hours, he continued to feel perplexed by what he had experienced. But then that night, when he lay in bed before sleeping, he suddenly had a sense of knowing that he was connected to the universe on some spiritual level. He realized that the peace he felt while floating was a message that he was being looked after and protected by a presence in the universe. And even though his scientific mind couldn't explain it, for Tim it was the first step in connecting with his own sense of spirituality.

Dianne was experiencing a health crisis. Her doctors told her that she needed to have back surgery to relieve some of her back pain, but the recovery would keep her out of work for weeks. Dianne kept delaying her surgery because she didn't want to do it. She had heard from some other people that the surgery wasn't always successful. Plus, she didn't want to miss work for such a lengthy period of time. Dianne wasn't sure what she should do. Spiritually, she was raised Jewish, but later in life she studied Buddhism and found great comfort in Buddhist artwork. Hung above her bed she had a traditional Tibetan painting of White Tara, a Buddhist deity who is said to restore health and protection in a person's life. Dianne had once been confident that her belief in alternative medicine, yoga, and the healing power of Tara could cure her pain, but after months of trying, nothing had improved. So she decided to try Deep Knowledge Meditation. She sat in her bedroom on a meditation cushion and used Still Mind Meditation to help her focus and relax. Then she began focusing on the image of White Tara and closed her eyes. She further concentrated on the sense of love and respect she felt toward Tara, and asked the question: "Should I have the surgery?" Before beginning Deep Knowledge Meditation, Dianne was convinced that she would be told not to have the surgery, but rather to put her trust in Tara's healing abilities. However, after a few minutes she began to see images in her mind's eye that startled her. She saw a scalpel, her doctor, and the surgery room. Then she saw images of the surgeon and herself smiling as well as images of herself walking without pain. The message appeared to be telling her to follow through with the surgery. This was not what Dianne expected or wanted to see, and it made her feel uneasy. But still, she offered thanks to White Tara when her meditation was complete and recorded her answer in the "Deep Knowledge Meditation Log." Over the next week, she did Deep Knowledge Meditation two more times, and the answers she received kept telling her the same thing. Dianne continued to wrestle with her decision, but she could no longer deny that her spiritual source of wisdom was telling her to have the surgery. So, reluctantly, Dianne scheduled the procedure.

Getting Answers to Your Spiritual Questions

For some people, using Deep Knowledge Meditation to connect with something bigger than themselves is going to feel like praying to a traditional God for answers. But Deep

Knowledge Meditation is different, because we're suggesting that you try sending your request for guidance to *any* spiritual source you think will be helpful. In fact, you might even try sending different requests to more than one source in order to determine which ones are easiest and clearest to access.

Building Your Practice:

- In addition to helping you turn inward for wisdom, Deep Knowledge Meditation can also be used to help you connect across the plane of existence with your spiritual sources of guidance.

- Begin by identifying a question and be as specific as possible.

- Then identify the best spiritual source to ask for guidance, and remember, it's possible that you might have different spiritual sources for help with different types of questions.

- Use Still Mind Meditation to help you relax and focus.

- Then use your imagination to help you connect with your spiritual source of wisdom; but most importantly, focus on the emotions of love and respect that you have for your spiritual source.

- After establishing an emotional connection of love and respect, ask your question.

- Be open to whatever response you receive, even if it's confusing or not the response you were hoping to get; responses can come as pictures, feelings, words, emotions, or even as a general principle, rather than a specific set of instructions.

- If you received no answer at all, consider rephrasing your question or asking a different spiritual source for guidance, and try again.

- When you're finished, offer thanks to your spiritual source of guidance.

- Finally, record your answers and possible future actions in the "Deep Knowledge Meditation Log," so that you can keep a record of your responses.

Chapter 9

Barriers to Living Your Spiritual Values

As you've already seen, growing toward spirit isn't a passive or merely contemplative process. It isn't enough to want spiritual growth. It isn't enough to pray or meditate and wait for some transformative process to unfold. Spiritual growth is active—it comes from things we do and choices we make. It's the product of *living* our mission and spiritual values.

Barriers to Values and Mission

What blocks access to spirit isn't the failure to perform practices, such as prayer and meditation, or going to church, temple, or ashram—it's the failure to live out our spiritual intentions. Here's the core problem: every step we take in a valued direction, every mission-based action, has the potential to generate painful feelings and thoughts. That's because acting on spiritual values usually involves choices that challenge us in some way, that require effort, that are not "the easy way." A commitment to pain avoidance often leads us away from values and mission for just this reason—values-based actions cost something. Consider the following examples:

James and the value of kindness. *At work, James is part of a task group developing strategic plans for his company. Two colleagues are contributing ideas that he feels are at best misguided, and possibly dangerous. His normal response is sarcasm, with a point-by-point rundown on what's wrong with their proposals. Acting on his value of kindness is hard for him. It requires controlling his anger and facing the anxiety that their notions will somehow win the day. It means facing the frustration of discussing "idiocies" and accepting the fact that his ideas are sometimes criticized in favor of theirs. He also has a sense of loss regarding his leadership role as he kindly welcomes and makes room for his colleagues to offer new directions. Notice how many uncomfortable feelings stand in the way of James's kindness: anxiety, the drive to express anger, frustration, and loss. It's no wonder that James, who has always wanted to be kind, has struggled to be so at work.*

Tammy and the value of listening. *Tammy's husband complains that he often feels alone in their relationship. Tammy, on the other hand, feels harried by numerous responsibilities and feels that she has heard everything her husband has to say already. He isn't full of surprises. Her value of taking time to listen and connect to him is challenging. She must somehow cope with the anxiety that important things aren't getting done, irritation and sometimes boredom as he describes the same feelings and concerns, and a familiar judgment that she has married a very "ordinary" man. Tammy has to face significant distress with her new commitment to have "face time" with her husband every day after work.*

Laura and the value of being of service. *Laura retired as a hospital floor nurse because of severe arthritis, but her need to be of service continues as she volunteers at a large homeless shelter, where she does medical screening. Every day she goes, Laura has to face serious physical pain and sadness about her condition. Further, she is frequently disturbed by the condition of the shelter residents and their sometimes hostile behavior. It costs her, but she shows up three mornings a week.*

Dale and the Compassion Meditation. *Dale grew up in an angry family. Now he periodically has angry meltdowns with his kids, and also feels a lot of anger at himself. He was reminded of his value of compassion when exposed to the Compassion*

Meditation, and committed to doing it daily. Now he has to face barriers before and during each meditation: tiredness, thoughts that it's a lot of effort and probably won't help, angry thoughts about his kids, sadness about his past and how "messed up" he is, and a certain amount of struggle to just stay with it.

The Four Barriers

In summary, most choices you make in a direction of values and mission will require you to face pain of some sort. That's why living in alignment with spirit can be hard and requires commitment. There are four barriers that get in the way of acting on values and mission: emotional barriers, thought barriers, unwillingness, and lack of clear intention/commitment. Let's look at each and see how they block our path.

Emotional barriers. The biggest emotional barrier to acting on spiritual values is usually fear—the fear of pain, the fear of failure, the fear of rejection, or the fear that something will be lost. And as you've seen in the examples, there are other emotional barriers, as well: frustration, shame, sadness, anger, boredom, emptiness, regret, and so on. Being able to name emotional barriers that you encounter is important because it makes them easier to recognize and face. Knowing what's in your way is essential to overcoming it.

Thought barriers. When something is hard to do (such as acting on values and mission), our minds often view it as a threat and try to discourage us from doing it. We may find our minds *predicting* dire outcomes if we carry out values-based intentions. Or our minds may have *judgments* that we're being stupid or are letting people take advantage of us. Our minds may dredge up failures from the past and predict they'll happen again, lashing us with self-attacks. As Dale found, our minds may tell us that values-based choices won't do any good.

Negative thoughts come part and parcel with the painful emotions described earlier. And as with emotions, noticing and labeling your painful thoughts helps you recognize them as barriers—even as you move forward with values-based choices. A barrier that's seen and identified is a barrier that can be overcome.

Unwillingness. When we are able to accept and face pain in service to our spiritual values, it's called *willingness*. The opposite, of course, is *unwillingness*—acting on values only if it doesn't hurt, only if we don't have to face pain. Unwillingness to feel pain makes it impossible to surmount emotional or thought barriers.

Willingness grows from acceptance—knowing and making room for the fact that some pain is inevitable as we move toward our values. Willingness doesn't mean that you want pain or won't try to get away from avoidable distress. It just means that when it's a choice between pain avoidance and your values, you'll choose values and accept whatever pain may come with them.

Lack of clear intentions. Acting on your spiritual values requires the clear intention to do so. As a reminder, an intention is a commitment to do a particular values-based action at a particular time and place. An intention always involves willingness because you are committed, no matter what barriers arise, no matter what the distress or cost.

Without a daily commitment to your intentions, you are likely either to forget them or lose willingness. Turning your values and mission into action is best achieved by making a determined plan—before beginning each day—so you'll see the moment of choice when it arises.

Noticing the Barriers

For the next week (or two if this process goes slowly) we'd like you to observe barriers that show up. At the end of each day, review moments when you acted on—or planned to act on—your intentions. Record what happened in the "Barriers Assessment Worksheet" on the next page. (You can download a PDF of the worksheet at http://www.newharbinger.com/43379.)

In column 1—Intentions—describe in a few words a recent values-based intention. For example, "Write a supportive email to my son." In column 2, note any negative emotions—even small ones—that occurred. For example, "Guilt at not writing earlier." In column 3, list barrier thoughts that are triggered by this intention. For example, "I'm a neglectful dad." In the fourth column—under "Willingness"—put a check mark if you were *willing* to have these thoughts and feel these emotions. Leave it blank if they were too hard to face. Finally, under "Commitment" in column 5, check if you formed a clear commitment to this intention. Leave it blank if you didn't make a Morning Intention.

Barrier Assessment Worksheet

INTENTIONS	EMOTIONS	THOUGHTS	WILLINGNESS	COMMITMENT

Barrier Assessment Worksheet

Example: Tammy's Week

INTENTIONS	EMOTIONS	THOUGHTS	WILLINGNESS	COMMITMENT
Telling Elena I was wrong; apologizing.	Shame, fear of her anger/rejection.	"There's no point. She won't accept it."	X	X
Helping Ginny with her homework every night without anger.	Exhausted, sick of it; resentment; want to walk away.	"She doesn't care; why should I? Can't stand her attitude."	X	X
Enroll for my x-ray tech certificate.	Fear of failure. Fear husband will get mad, feel neglected.	"Too much work. I'll never finish. Too brain dead. Waste of time."	X	X
Talk to my husband about his work.	Boredom; regret; stress about things I need to do; irritation.	"It's going to be the same old, same old. He's such a complainer, so ordinary."		
Help husband with doing his books (at work) in a supportive way.	Resentment, impatient with his accounting system and handwriting; tired.	"Why do I have to do this just because he can't?"	X	X
Give Ginny more affection—hug her every day; say "I love you."	Feels phony; feel resentment about her lack of affection for me.	"She doesn't care."	X	
Do a walking meditation to get more peaceful and centered on Monday and Thursday.	Anxious about what I need to do; harried, tired, discouraged about the amount of effort.	Sad thoughts about myself; things I've lost or never done.	X	
Call Isabel, who's been sick.	Anxious about things I should be doing; fear of cancer.		X	
Call my mother.	Boredom; resentment.	"There's nothing to say."		

Key Barrier Themes

After you've kept the "Barrier Assessment Worksheet" for a week or two, some themes may surface that are worth noting and that may help with follow-through on future intentions. You may find that intentions in a certain category elicit characteristic emotions. For example, when Tammy set goals that involved helping people, she often had to face the barrier of resentment. Likewise, multiple intentions focused on the same person may trigger similar emotional and thought barriers. Again, Tammy had the same thought ("She doesn't care") across several intentions with her daughter.

On your "Barrier Assessment Worksheet" put a check next to intentions that you carried out. Is there a pattern here? You may notice, as Tammy did, that goals with no clear intention (commitment) or willingness don't happen. While Tammy had a vague idea, each night, that she would chat with her husband, she never did. A lack of willingness is almost always going to block your intentions—unless the emotional cost is very small. It's probably not worth making an intention unless you feel willing to face whatever pain it might bring.

For most people, making a clear commitment—every day—to enact your intention greatly increases the chance for follow-through. Does your experience bear this out? If so, committed intentions, each morning, may help turn your values and mission into action. Are there certain emotions and thoughts that are more likely to block your intentions than others? Make note of these. They are high obstacles you'll need to anticipate and plan for. Tammy noticed, for example, that any intention triggering fear or resentment was a much harder climb. She needed more willingness to hold these emotions while acting on spiritual values.

Overcoming Barriers to Spiritual Values

The path to spiritual growth must always climb past the obstacle of pain. There are four ways to surmount emotional and thought barriers: acceptance, remembering life purpose and mission, Deep Knowledge Meditation, and Daily Intentions.

Acceptance. Acceptance is allowing. It's permitting whatever painful thoughts and feelings you have to be there: to notice them without resistance or avoidance, and to observe them while not overengaging—without trying to figure them out, trying to understand why, or wondering where it will all end.

Acceptance is letting whatever emotion or thought shows up to be there, however intensely experienced, until the next emotion or thought takes its place. Acceptance lies at the heart of willingness. When you accept an emotion without resistance, you are willing to have it. In fact, accepting any unavoidable pain—letting it be there without trying to change it—*is* willingness.

One of the most effective ways to cultivate acceptance is to practice a meditation we call, simply, Acceptance Meditation. The instructions follow. It will help you make room for any form of discomfort—emotional, mental, or physical. Try this meditation right now. Most people find it relaxing, even in the face of pain. We encourage you to make it a part of your daily spiritual practice. Simply add it to the Still Mind Meditation that you already do each day.

Acceptance Meditation Instructions

You can practice this meditation whenever you feel distressed in your daily life. If you prefer to listen to the instructions, first record them on your smartphone.

To begin, find a place where you won't be disturbed for at least fifteen minutes. Turn off the ringer on your smartphone. Find a comfortable position to relax, whether you're sitting or lying down. Then use Still Mind Meditation to help you breathe and focus for two to three minutes. Allow your belly to gently expand as you breathe in and effortlessly collapse as you breathe out. Find a slow, natural rhythm of breathing and allow your body and mind to relax. Establish your breath as the center of your awareness. *(Pause here for two to three minutes if you're recording these instructions.)*

When you are ready, discover where the stress or difficult emotion manifests in your body. You might notice tension, pain, an itch, or just a strange sensation in your body. Just notice it without judging it, and place your attention there for a minute. *(Pause here if recording the instructions.)*

Next, *soften* toward that stress or difficult emotion in your body. Allow the muscles to release around it. Just notice the feeling or emotion without trying to control or push it away. Your body can be soft around the edges of the feeling, making room for it. Letting go...letting go...letting go of tension around the edges of the feeling. *(Pause here if recording the instructions.)*

As you're observing, if you experience too much discomfort from an emotion, just do your best to note your experience and return to the rising and falling of your breath; use your breath as your anchor. Do your best not to judge your emotion and not to get distracted by it. *(Pause here if recording the instructions.)*

Similarly, if a difficult thought arises, do your best to just notice it and let it go. Again, return to the rising and falling of your breath as your anchor. Do your best not to judge yourself or the thought. *(Pause here if recording the instructions.)*

Now *hold* the feeling or emotion kindly. Move your hand to cover and hold the spot. Breathe into that feeling; breathe in a kind regard for that stress or difficult emotion. Think of this place as yours to take care of, to hold as if it were precious and needing your love. *(Pause here if recording the instructions.)*

Again, if a difficult thought arises, or your mind wanders, notice and accept it. Then let it go. *(Pause here if recording the instructions.)*

Finally, let this feeling or emotion be. *Let it be* there without resistance. Let it go or stay. Let it change or not change. Let it be where it is or move. Let it be what it is, making room for it, holding it, accepting its presence in your body and your life. *(Pause here if recording the instructions.)*

Soften...hold...let be. Soften...hold...let be. Soften...hold...let be. Repeat these words to yourself, holding any pain you may have kindly. Allowing it to stay or leave or change. *(Pause here if recording the instructions.)*

As you continue, allow difficult thoughts to arise—just noticing them and letting them go. *(Pause here if recording the instructions.)*

As you continue, you may find that the emotion moves in your body, or even changes into another emotion. Try staying with your experience, continuing to use the technique of Soften-Hold-Let Be. *(Pause here if recording the instructions.)*

Finally, return your attention to your breath, simply noticing the rising and falling of your breath: breath in and breath out. Then, when you are ready, slowly open your eyes when you're done. *(Stop recording the instructions.)*

(This acceptance meditation is inspired by Christopher Germer and Kristin Neff's "Soften, Soothe, Allow" meditation, found at https://selfcompassion.org/category/exercises/#guided-meditations.)

Remembering your life purpose and mission. The second way to overcome barriers is to remember your life's mission. What are you here to do and learn? What is your life about?

If you haven't done so already, condense the "Life Mission Statement" you developed in chapter 6 into a single sentence. Now, each morning when you do Daily Intentions, recall your mission—captured in that single sentence. Write it here:

_____

_____

_____

_____

_____

Our life mission (including the spiritual values that emerge from it) is what gives us the strength and motivation to overcome barriers to spirit. We need a big reason to face pain. Our mission and purpose in living is that reason. Try to connect each of your values-based intentions to your mission *before undertaking them.* Having a clear idea of why you're doing something is the surest way to make certain it happens. And when barriers show up, always recall your mission because this is your core motivation for every values-based choice you make.

Deep Knowledge Meditation. When barriers show up, you can use Deep Knowledge Meditation to do two things: First, you may want to confirm that your intention is aligned with spirit. Sometimes our intentions, even though they appear to be values-based, fall off the mark. They turn out to be driven by some other—sometimes self-serving—motivation.

The second way to use Deep Knowledge Meditation with barriers is to ask how best to face or overcome them. Just inquire: "How can I face or deal with [the barrier] while still doing [my intention]?" As with all your meditations that tap into spirit, the answer may come at once as a sudden "knowing" or show up later as a gradually emerging clarity or awareness. Either way, Deep Knowledge Meditation is a good resource when you're struggling with emotional and thought barriers.

Daily Intentions. You've used intentions before—to learn to recognize the moment of choice and to set values-based goals to be carried out at a specific time and place. Daily Intentions is a practice we encourage you to use each morning. Start your day by promising yourself to do these three things:

1. To live and make choices based on life mission and purpose. Recall your one-sentence mission statement. For example, "Everything I do comes from love."

2. To look for opportunities this day to turn your intentions into actions. Recall or identify specific intentions that you plan to carry out. See if you can determine when and where these might happen throughout the day. Examples from Tammy:

   a. Half-hour check-in with my husband about his day after work.

   b. Calling Isabel about how she's doing with chemotherapy.

   c. Helping Ginny with her homework in a supportive, nonexasperated way.

   d. Giving Ginny a hug before school this morning and telling her—in a real rather than offhand way—that I love her.

   e. Apologizing to Elena first thing this morning at work.

   f. Walking meditation at lunch.

3. To look for opportunities this day to turn your intentions into commitments. You are likely to find, as Tammy did, that making Daily Intentions helps you to face barriers and actually carry out most of your spiritual goals. An intention is really a *commitment*; making Morning Intentions is making the commitment, each day, to act in alignment with spirit.

Keeping Track

You've learned about barriers and how to cope with them. Now it's time to track how you do. The "Barriers Log" on the next page is designed to be used once or twice a week to record what happens with your most important values and intentions. You may want to make copies of the blank log so you can do additional entries over time. (You can download a PDF of the log at http://www.newharbinger.com/43379.)

List your most cherished values in the left-hand column—one in each box. Under "Intentions," list one to three key intentions *for each value*. As an example, for Tammy's value of being loving and supportive, she now listed several intentions regarding her daughter and husband. Across from the value of honesty, she listed an intention to apologize to her coworker and to call her brother (who was hurt about something she had said).

Now, in the next column ("Barriers"), identify whatever significant barriers showed up as you either planned for or turned your intention into action—noting one or two words for thoughts or emotions.

Finally comes the most important column: "Actions." What did you do? The choice is always: trying to get away from painful thoughts and feelings versus acting on values. Just write "Yes" or "No" as to whether you carried out your values-based intention. One more thing should be noted under "Actions"—what did you do to deal with barriers? Make a brief note if you tried acceptance/willingness, remembering life mission, Deep Knowledge Meditation, Daily Intentions, or anything else to deal with the emotions and thoughts that threatened to derail intended action.

Barriers Log

MOST IMPORTANT VALUES	INTENTIONS	BARRIERS	ACTIONS

Keep the "Barriers Log" for as long as it seems useful. Remember, what you notice and monitor helps you change. What you don't notice or keep track of *can't change*. Growing spiritually depends on being aware of what you do and using that knowledge to make better decisions—choices more aligned with spirit.

Building Your Practice:

- The barriers to acting on values are painful feelings and thoughts, unwillingness to face that pain, and a lack of clear intentions.

- Overcoming barriers requires acceptance of pain and willingness to face painful feelings and thoughts (Acceptance Meditation), staying mindful of your life mission, seeking wisdom via Deep Knowledge Meditation, and practicing Daily Intentions.

- Continue daily your Still Mind Meditation and Compassion Meditation.

- Continue Daily Intentions each morning.

- Use Deep Knowledge Meditation whenever needed.

- Complete the "Barriers Log" one or two times per week.

Chapter 10

Compassion for Self and Others

Having just explored the barriers to living your spiritual values, in this chapter, you'll learn to strengthen a force that can surmount those barriers—compassion. Compassion is a state of mind that recognizes the universality of pain in human experience. We are all in this difficult life together, all experiencing losses, hurts, and the realization that so many things are not as we wish them to be. Compassion is the recognition that we are connected by our common humanity, this shared experience of hope and pain. Compassion is also the acceptance of that pain—for ourselves and others—and appreciating that pain without judgment or fault. Lastly, compassion has, at its core, the *intention* that all who suffer find peace and well-being.

Compassion is both awareness (of the common struggle we all face) and an active intention to heal whatever hurts. It is, at the same time, seeing and caring for all who share this difficult life. It is love.

Why Compassion Is Important

Compassion lifts us beyond the judgmental thoughts that paralyze us and make it so difficult at times to act on our values. Those thoughts are softened by a *compassionate mind* that does not blame us for our suffering. Rather, compassion helps us accept the struggle that all of us on this planet must experience.

Compassion lightens our emotional load. Self-hate and regret fade away. The sense of being wrong and bad loses its power. And the feeling of being alone in our pain and vulnerability is transformed into being part of the human community.

Compassion for Others

Compassion for others—seeing, appreciating, and wanting to heal their pain—lies at the root of kindness and love, and brings us closer to spirit. The Compassion for Others Meditation below can be added to your Still Mind Meditation, and should be a daily practice.

Notice that this meditation includes compassion for someone you care for as well as someone you find difficult, perhaps even repugnant. The ability to extend compassion, regardless of likeability or personality type, is crucial to strengthening your compassion "muscle." Selective compassion won't help you grow spiritually. Having compassion for the people you don't like—seeing their pain and wishing it healed—is how we learn to extend love and caring.

Compassion for Others Meditation

After a period of Still Mind Meditation, place your hand over your heart, feeling the warmth and gentle pressure of your hand....Now bring to mind a person who makes you smile, who naturally brings happiness to your heart....Let yourself feel what it's like to be in that person's presence....Now recognize that this person wants to be happy and free of suffering. As you hold that awareness, mentally repeat the following phrases, letting them be a deep wish:

May you be peaceful.

May you be safe.

May you be healthy.

May you be happy and free of suffering.

Now bring to mind the image of a difficult and disliked person. Remind yourself that this difficult person is struggling to find his or her way through life, even though in doing so he or she may be causing you pain. Mentally repeat: *Just as I want to be peaceful and free from suffering...*

May you, too, find peace.

May you be safe.

May you be healthy.

May you be happy and free of suffering.

For the next week, make this part of your Still Mind Meditation practice. Then, see if you can bring it into your daily interactions with people. Say to yourself with each encounter:

Just like me, they want to be happy and free of suffering, or

Just like me, these people walking past are caught in the drama and flow of life.

Finally, you may want to abbreviate these mantras to the simple phrase: "Just like me."

Self-Compassion

Many people find self-compassion harder than compassion for others. That's why we suggest doing the Compassion for Others Meditation first, before attempting to direct compassion inward. The challenges of self-compassion include:

- Self-compassion requires us to be in contact with our own pain. We have to acknowledge how much we hurt, how human and vulnerable we are. For many people, awareness of their own suffering feels scary or wrong or self-indulgent. It may threaten the denial that keeps pain a safe distance away. But here's the problem: if you have no awareness of your pain, you can feel no empathy or kindness toward yourself. And you feel disconnected from our common human struggle.

- The self-hating voice drowns out compassion. Many of us have a pathological critic inside, born of parental attacks and hurtful rejections. We use that critical voice to perfect ourselves, to try to be better. But the self-hating voice just crushes our sense of worth and makes us deaf to compassion. We don't think we deserve it.

- A sense of self-subjugation. Many people grow up with a sense that *others* are more deserving, that their needs come first. Through the lens of love, the needs of others are always important, but every soul has great value and deserves care. Self-subjugation makes compassion for yourself impossible because you don't seem to be important. Your pain and needs don't seem to matter.

- Fear that you'll lose accountability. Some people are afraid that self-compassion will take them off the hook for their faults, and that they'll stop trying to be good. Because compassion is a large part of self-forgiveness, people fear that forgiving themselves is excusing themselves.

- Self-compassion isn't supported by Judeo-Christian orthodoxy, where the main concern is not doing wrong, not sinning. Religions often use shame and a fear of being cast out for social control. Self-compassion flies in the face of shame; it accepts mistakes because they are how we learn.

- Self-compassion embraces the "whole you," not just the "good you." We often divide ourselves into good and bad, rejecting the shadow parts that we wish weren't there. This creates a damaging internal divide that only compassion can heal.

Self-Compassion Meditation

You can add this meditation into your daily practice, now comprising the Still Mind Meditation, the Compassion for Others Meditation, and the Self-Compassion Meditation. When you have completed the Compassion for Others Meditation, add the following:

Now bring your awareness inside your own body, noting the world of sensation there at this very moment. You live in this body—let yourself be aware of your breath, your life force. As you hold this awareness, mentally repeat the phrases:

> May I be peaceful.
>
> May I be safe.
>
> May I be healthy.
>
> May I be happy and free of suffering.

Putting It All Together

The two Compassion Meditations are joined in a complete script on the next page. If you wish, you can record it on your smartphone and use it whenever you are doing your daily practices.

Script for Other-Compassion and Self-Compassion Meditations

After you have done the Still Mind Meditation...

Now place your hand over your heart, feeling the warmth and gentle pressure of your hand. (Pause here for a few seconds.) Now bring to mind a person who makes you smile, who naturally brings happiness to your heart. (Again, pause here for a few seconds.) Let yourself feel what it's like to be in that person's presence. (Pause here for a minute.) Now recognize that that person wishes to be happy and free of suffering. As you hold that awareness, mentally repeat the following phrases, letting them be a deep wish:

May you be peaceful.

May you be safe.

May you be healthy.

May you be happy and free from suffering.

Now bring to mind the image of a difficult person. (Pause here for a few seconds.) Remind yourself that this difficult person is also struggling to find his or her way through life. (Pause here for a few seconds.) He or she is also suffering. (Pause here for a few seconds.) And in doing so, he or she is also causing you pain. (Pause here for a few seconds.) Mentally repeat: "Just as I wish to be peaceful and free from suffering..."

May you too find peace.

May you too be safe.

May you too be healthy.

May you too be happy and free from suffering.

Now bring your awareness inside your own body, noting the world of sensation there at this very moment. (Pause here for a few seconds.) You live in this body—let yourself be aware of your breath, your life force. (Pause here for a few seconds.) As you hold that awareness, mentally repeat the following phrase, pausing for a few seconds after each ones:

May I be peaceful.

May I be safe.

May I be healthy.

May I be happy and free from suffering.

Finally, taking a few slow breaths, rest quietly and savor the good will and compassion on which you were just focused.

Noticing with Gratitude

Achieving compassion in daily life means putting the intentions of your meditations into action. One good way to do this is to *notice* when compassion and kindness are sent your way. Each day, as part of your Morning Intention, commit to noticing acts of kindness. And when you see them, pause to experience gratitude. Mentally or verbally thank whoever gave you that gift. Noticing and appreciating compassion makes it a real part of your life. It becomes something that matters and gets woven more and more into your relationships. Examples of kindness that are often overlooked include: receiving a compliment; someone asking how you are doing; someone giving you an unexpected smile; someone offering you unasked-for help; someone giving you small gifts of their time and effort; someone noticing when you are distressed or in a bad mood; or even another driver making room for you to move into his lane.

It often helps to write down your gratitude in the form of a journal, or to simply make a list of appreciations at the end of the day. Making written notes of your gratitude can have the effect of triggering compassion and appreciation for the support you receive from others.

The Compassion Awareness Journal

For the next week, keep a record of moments when you felt compassion—for yourself or someone else. As you'll see on the next page, the first step is to make a note describing the situation that triggered your compassion. What exactly happened? What allowed this feeling to bloom? Next, take a look at how compassion felt to you in this situation. There's a checklist and space to write the unique details of your experience. The last question asks what you did. Was there a way you turned compassion into action? Did you smile and nod? Give a hug? Do some small kindness? Stop to listen? If there was self-compassion, did you pause to appreciate and validate your own struggle? Did you ask for support? Did you tell someone what you're going through? When there isn't a compassionate action, that's okay. Make no judgment about it. But be aware that a compassionate action is often possible and grows from the intention that you and others be free of suffering. (You can download a PDF of the journal template at http://www.newharbinger.com/43379.)

Compassion Awareness Journal

1. The situation—what triggered your compassion? _____

    _____

    _____

2. What did you feel?

    ☐ Common humanity; shared experience

    ☐ Acceptance and nonjudgment

    ☐ Desire to give or receive kindness

    ☐ Sense of love

    ☐ Intention for happiness and relief from suffering

Other feelings: _____

    _____

3. What did you do? _____

    _____

    _____

1. The situation—what triggered your compassion? _____

    _____

    _____

2. What did you feel?

☐ Common humanity; shared experience

☐ Acceptance and nonjudgment

☐ Desire to give or receive kindness

☐ Sense of love

☐ Intention for happiness and relief from suffering

Other feelings: _____

_____

3. What did you do? _____

_____

_____

1. The situation—what triggered your compassion? _____

_____

_____

2. What did you feel?

☐ Common humanity; shared experience

☐ Acceptance and nonjudgment

☐ Desire to give or receive kindness

☐ Sense of love

☐ Intention for happiness and relief from suffering

Other feelings: _____

_____

3. What did you do? _____

_____

_____

1. The situation—what triggered your compassion? _____

_____

_____

2. What did you feel?

☐ Common humanity; shared experience

☐ Acceptance and nonjudgment

☐ Desire to give or receive kindness

☐ Sense of love

☐ Intention for happiness and relief from suffering

Other feelings: _____

_____

3. What did you do? _____

_____

_____

Leonardo's Compassion Awareness Journal

1.   The situation—what triggered your compassion? *Walking home, I saw a little boy playing alone in his front yard—it reminded me of how lonely I felt as a kid. The boy seemed kind of lost and sad.*

2.   What did you feel?

   ☑ Common humanity; shared experience

   ☑ Acceptance and nonjudgment

   ☑ Desire to give or receive kindness

   ☐ Sense of love

   ☑ Intention for happiness and relief from suffering

Other feelings: *I felt a sense of pride that I'd survived my childhood, and a deep sadness for how much children suffer, including this little boy.*

3. What did you do? *He had a ball and was throwing it up to catch it. I stopped and said he was good at catching the ball. I asked him about stuff he likes to do, and he told me soccer (he wanted to get on a team). We kept talking for a while and I urged him to find a team.*

1.   The situation—what triggered your compassion? *I was reading a sad book and I realized what a familiar emotion it is, how sadness so often seems like an undernote in my life.*

2.   What did you feel?

   ☐ Common humanity; shared experience

   ☑ Acceptance and nonjudgment

   ☑ Desire to give or receive kindness

   ☑ Sense of love

   ☑ Intention for happiness and relief from suffering

Other feelings: *Just kind of allowing the sadness, visiting with it like an old friend.*

3.   What did you do? *I decided to soothe myself—pulled up the Leonard Cohen song: "Everybody Knows That's the Way It Goes." It felt like Cohen understood my sadness.*

Building Your Practice:

- Compassion, whether for self or others, involves a recognition of the universality of pain in human experience, an acceptance of that pain without judgment, and the intention that all people find peace from suffering.

- Compassion can be fostered and strengthened by the Self-Compassion Meditation and the Compassion for Others Meditation, both of which should be included in your daily meditation practice.

- You can also foster compassion by noticing with gratitude when compassion arises, journaling (for at least a week) about situations triggering your compassion, and turning compassion into (small) actions.

- Continue using Deep Knowledge Meditation as situations arise that require wise choices. Spirit will help you if you ask.

- Continue your Morning Intentions to recognize the moments of choice and identify the opportunities during the day to enact your values-based intentions. When barriers arise, use your "Barriers Log" to plan a way through.

Chapter 11

Making Amends

In the previous chapter, you learned about expressing compassion for yourself and others. When you act compassionately, you recognize that someone is hurting and you take action to help relieve some of that pain. Literally, the word *compassion* means "together in suffering." But being compassionate toward others is often easier when we ourselves were not the cause of the person's pain.

So what happens when you *are* the cause of someone else's suffering? For many of us, it's very hard to admit that we have caused someone else's pain. As a result, we often avoid the subject and hope it goes away. We avoid the person, the subject of his or her pain, and anything else that reminds us of what we did to that person. But unfortunately, avoidance doesn't make the other person's pain go away; in fact, it often creates pain for the person who caused the suffering as well. If you caused someone else pain, you may feel guilty, remorseful, angry, sad, or regret what you did—especially if you have never apologized for the pain you caused. In cases like these—where you were the cause of someone else's pain—it's often necessary to make amends.

Making amends is a form of compassion. But in many ways, it is a more difficult form of compassion to put into action. When you seek to make amends to someone, you have to join in that person's suffering, but you also have to admit that you caused that pain. Making amends is similar to apologizing, in that you often begin by saying, "I'm sorry." But making amends goes further by stating, "I see the suffering I have caused you and I'm offering my help to relieve you of that suffering as much as I can."

There is no shame in making amends. In fact, in some ways, it's one of the highest forms of compassion and love for others that you can demonstrate. We all make mistakes, and we all sometimes cause harm to other people. But it takes a very brave and honest person to admit his or her fault and to attempt to correct it.

Make Amends Without Judgments

Ideally, amends are made without judgment, neither of yourself nor of the other person. When you judge yourself or others—such as, "I'm bad" or "You were wrong for making me do what I did"—you cause even more pain and suffering. Judgments can also get in the way of your seeking to make amends in the first place. For example, someone might think, "Why would she want me to make amends anyway? I'm a jerk for hurting her." Or, conversely, "Why should I make amends, when he was being such a jerk that he provoked me to do it?" So, do your best not to judge yourself or anyone else. Don't let this discourage you from seeking to make amends in the first place.

Don't Expect to Erase the Past

It's also important to remember that just because you think you are ready to make amends to someone, that doesn't mean that the other person is ready to accept your apology, or especially to "forgive and forget." Do your best to make amends to someone you've hurt because it's the right thing to do, but don't expect miracles. Making amends is not going to erase the errors of the past and allow you to continue a relationship with another person as if nothing ever happened. But amends can allow you take spiritual responsibility for your actions, stay in alignment with your values, and create healthier, more loving relationships with other people.

Do I Need to Make Amends?

So how do you know if you need to make amends to someone? Sometimes the answer is obvious. If you've hurt someone—intentionally or not—in a physical, emotional, sexual, spiritual, or psychological manner, it's very likely that you need to make amends (although these are not the *only* things for which you need to make amends). Sometimes the impact of your harmful actions is obvious; for example, you physically hit someone and leave a mark, you yell at someone and make them cry, you threaten someone with your words and make them shake nervously, or you harm someone sexually and leave them feeling broken and depressed.

But many times we cause more subtle pain or pain that is not so easy to see. For example, you ignore your friend, you're rude to the woman at the checkout counter, you neglect spending quality time with your children, or you gossip about your coworkers. Every day, each of us makes mistakes and some of those mistakes cause harm to people. No matter how small the harm might seem to you, it's equally important to make amends for those offenses. Remember, making amends is not just about apologizing. The true purpose of making amends is to assist someone who is suffering and to help you live according to your spiritual values, which very likely includes forming healthier, happier relationships with other people.

In the Alcoholics Anonymous 12-step program for sobriety, the eighth step requires the participant to make a list of all the people whom he or she has harmed in order to make amends to them. This is a great idea, and one that you can use not only in your recovery from addiction, but also in your spiritual development. If you are already aware of some of the people you've harmed in the past, to whom you should make amends, then by all means make a list or use the "Amends Worksheet" near the end of this chapter.

Make an Honest Inventory of Your Past

If you're having a difficult time determining the people to whom you need to make amends, try this method. Begin with Still Mind Meditation and keep a pen and paper next to you. Quiet your mind and your body. Then begin mentally reviewing your life from the time you were a child until the present. Begin with ages six through ten. Ask yourself, "Who were the people I was close to? Did I bring them any harm?" Then ask yourself, "Were there others that I brought harm to for which I should make amends?" If any names or incidents come to mind, write them down. Then move on to the next five years of your life, from ages eleven through fifteen, and ask yourself the same questions, writing down any names or incidents that you remember. Continue reviewing your life in five-year increments until you get to your present age.

By the time you're done, you might have one name or you might have a hundred names. But again, do your best not to judge yourself about mistakes you've made in the past. This is not a shaming exercise. This is a mindfulness exercise to help you make an honest inventory of regrets, an honest assessment of your responsibilities, and an honest list of the people to whom you need to make amends.

How Do I Make Amends?

Now that you've identified the people whom you've harmed in some way, you need to learn how to make amends. There are five steps: (1) taking responsibility for your actions, (2) deciding on the conditions and content of how you are going to make amends, (3) creating intentions without any expectations, (4) making an atonement, and (5) making amends regularly.

Taking Responsibility

By this point, you've identified someone to whom you need to make amends. You were able to either make a list of people or you used the Still Mind Meditation technique to help you. In some way, you've already taken responsibility by admitting that you caused the other person harm. But it also might help to name the actions you took that caused that harm. Use the "Amends Worksheet" at the end of this exercise to help you.

In addition, if there are situations for which you are not sure if you are 100 percent responsible for the harm done, make an honest assessment of the amount of harm for which you were responsible. You can still make amends for even a small amount of harm done to another person.

Deciding on the Conditions and Content

Next, you need to decide how you're going to make amends and what you're going to say. The conditions for making amends can take many forms. This is "how" you're going to make amends, such as writing a letter, making a phone call, sending an email, or setting up a face-to-face meeting. When making your decision, consider what is going to be easiest for the person receiving the amends. For example, don't insist on a personal meeting if the person lives far away or if the last interaction with the person was very unpleasant. Also, allow the other person some privacy when making amends; for example, don't post an apology to her Facebook page for all of her friends and family to see.

Regarding the content of the amends, keep your statement simple, direct, and focused on what *you* did wrong. Use "I" statements, meaning, start your sentences with your actions, feelings, and responsibilities—not the other person's. For example, "I want to apologize because I realize I hurt you when I yelled at you last night at the restaurant. I now feel really upset and guilty about what I did and I want to take responsibility for my actions. I want to make it up to you in some way." Even if you are going to speak directly on the phone or meet face-to-face, write down what you are going to say and practice saying it. Keep it short, direct, and focused on your own actions—not what the other person did.

In addition, consider another good piece of advice from Alcoholics Anonymous: Do your best to make amends to someone you've harmed unless doing so would cause that person *more* harm. So again, think about the other person, not just yourself. For example, if you had an affair with someone who was married, and now you want to contact that person to make amends, but you suspect that person's spouse might find out if you do make contact, then don't do it! Again, be respectful of the other person's feelings and needs.

So, in cases where contacting another person might cause them more harm, or in the case of not being able to contact someone because he is either dead or living somewhere unknown, what can you do? One suggestion is to make the amends anyway, either on paper or saying the words out loud. Make your statement to the person's spirit or memory. You might also imagine what he would say in return and further make a commitment to his spirit or memory to take healthier values-based actions in the future. Make a pledge to change your own behavior to avoid someone else suffering in similar situations. Plus, if there is still some way to fix the harm you did, even in his absence, then you should consider doing so.

Creating Intentions without Expectations

Creating intentions without expectations means that you make amends without expecting anything in return. Period. Just because you are apologizing and offering to relieve the person of suffering in some way, that doesn't mean that the other person is going to listen to you, has to care, is going to accept your apology, or wants to repair the relationship. Making amends is not a guarantee that anything between you and the other person will change or improve.

And yet, our suggestion is that you should still do it. Why? Because making amends is like relieving yourself of a burden, a burden of knowing that you caused someone harm and failed to do anything about it. You stood by while the other person suffered in some way, and for many people who do this, their own actions often cause feelings of guilt, shame, anger, self-hatred, and depression. When we offer amends, there is often an unburdening of those feelings. It is like a spiritual detoxification process. So, in addition to making an offer to help relieve the other person of suffering, making amends can help you feel better too.

Atonement

An atonement is a commitment you make in response to your harmful actions. You make an offer to the other person to help relieve her suffering somehow, or you promise to change something about yourself so that you won't commit that same type of harm in the future—to avoid additional future suffering.

Making Amends Regularly

Finally, the last step of making amends is to engage in the practice regularly. Making amends is an ongoing process that should be a part of your daily spiritual practice. Recognizing your mistakes and making amends is an integral part of your spiritual growth. Ideally, with practice, you will begin to notice more quickly when you have harmed someone and you will make amends more quickly too.

On the following page is a blank "Amends Worksheet" to help you work through your own amends-making process. After that are some examples of making amends. (You can download a PDF of the worksheet at http://www.newharbinger.com/43379.)

Amends Worksheet

To whom do I need to make amends? _____

What actions am I responsible for? _____

_____

_____

_____

How will I contact the person? _____

_____

_____

What will I say to the person? (Use "I" statements.)

My actions ("I'm sorry for what I did when I...") _____

_____

_____

My feelings ("I feel...") _____

_____

My responsibilities ("I'm responsible for my actions, including...") _____

_____

_____

My atonement to relieve suffering ("I would like to help you by...") _____

_____

_____

Examples of Making Amends

Jeremy ended a relationship with his girlfriend, Anne, five years ago—without telling her why. The truth was that he had an affair with someone else, but he always felt guilty as a result of his actions. He still had Anne's email address and followed her on Twitter. So as part of his spiritual development, Jeremy made a commitment to make amends to Anne. He decided that the best, most private way to make amends was to send her a private email. He simply wrote: "Hi Anne, this is Jeremy. I hope you are well. I know this might sound weird, but I'm writing to apologize to you for my actions five years ago when I ended our relationship. I don't expect us to get back together or anything. I just wanted you to know that I was wrong for what I did. I was actually having an affair with someone else, and I am so ashamed of myself now for what I did. I take full responsibility for my actions and for hurting your feelings. If there is anything I can do at this point to correct my actions, please let me know. Otherwise, please know that I've made a commitment to never hurt anyone like that ever again. I'm very sorry, Jeremy."

Jessica was a mother of three adult children, but when they were younger, Jessica struggled with addiction and neglected her children. As a result, they were estranged from her. Now, as Jessica was getting older and had found sobriety, she wanted to reconnect with her children and hopefully get to know them better. She no longer had their addresses, but she knew someone who did, and that friend promised to pass along any letters that Jessica wanted to send. Jessica sent them each the following letter: "Dear children. I just wanted to tell each of you that I am sorry for my actions when you were younger, growing up. I was not a good mother to you, and for that I am truly, truly sorry. My addiction got the best of me and made me neglect you. That is not an excuse for my actions, but I want you to know that I have been sober now for nine months. I feel so sad inside because I know that I wasted my life and never got a chance to know you or treat you like a good mother should. I take 100 percent responsibility for my actions in the past. But now I am hoping that I can make it up to you in the future somehow. I can promise each of you, that if you give me another chance, I will come to visit each of you and do my best to correct my past behavior."

Michael was rude to the woman behind the checkout counter in the supermarket. Last week he was in a hurry, and in his rush, he told the woman that she was moving too slowly and should be fired. He said it loud enough for several other people to hear. The woman didn't say anything, but Michael knew he hurt her feelings and he wanted to make amends. He thought about calling the store, but he didn't want to embarrass the woman, so he decided to write a small note and keep it in his wallet for the next time he saw her. Finally, one afternoon, Michael saw the same woman working behind the checkout counter and he waited in her line. She didn't seem to remember him, but when he got to the front of the line, Michael whispered, "I'm sorry," and handed her the note. Here's what it said: "My name is Michael and I am really sorry about what I said the last time I saw you. I had no right to yell at you in front of other people and to say that you should be fired. I was totally in the wrong, and in a bad mood and I took it out on you. I hope this makes up for my rudeness." Attached to the note was a $25 gift certificate to a local restaurant.

Jennifer wanted to make amends to her father, but unfortunately her father passed away over fifteen years ago. The last time she had seen him alive, they had argued, and Jennifer said she never wanted to speak with him again. So she didn't call him for several months, and then he suddenly died. Since his death, Jennifer has felt guilt-ridden about her actions and the fact that she never got a chance to apologize. She decided that she was going to make amends to his spirit, which she believed continued to survive. She initially wrote out her statement of amends but then decided to read it out loud as if he were standing in the room with her. "Dad, I'm very, very sorry for what I said to you. I said many mean things to you that day, over fifteen years ago, especially 'You're not a good father' and 'I never want to speak to you ever again.' I am so sorry, and I regret saying those words every day of my life. You had nothing to do with my saying those things, that was my mistake. I know I can't make it up to you now, but I want you to know that since then I've made a commitment to my husband, my children, and my friends to tell them how much I love them every day and how important they are to me. I am so sorry for what I did." Then she closed her eyes and imagined her father standing in the room. She saw him smile at her, hug her, and kiss her. Then he said, "It's okay," and Jennifer felt a sense of relief wash over her.

More Examples of Making Amends

Several years ago, we, the authors, sitting at a dinner table, discussed making amends to people we had known—people to whom we had acted unkindly in our pasts. All of the people we wanted to make amends to we had not spoken to in decades. So at that time we made a pact to contact some of those people, using the method outlined above. (We had originally conceptualized writing an entire book about making amends, so we wanted to see what would happen.) The results were amazing. One of us contacted a person on the phone and then had dinner with that same person. Again, this was a person who had not been seen in decades. Over the course of the meal, past wrongs had been forgiven and the friendship was rekindled. The person who was wronged received an apology, but in addition, the author felt a great sense of relief, like a heavy burden had been removed after many years. Similarly, the other author decided to contact three people, via email, with a message similar to this one: "Dear XXX, I was talking with a friend recently about making amends to people I've hurt and your name came to mind as someone I owed an apology to. So, I just wanted to say that I'm sorry for any pain that I caused you all those years ago. I don't expect a reply from you, nor do I expect this to reconnect our friendship. I just wanted you to know that I regret some of the ways I treated you many years ago. I hope you and your family are well." Again, the results were amazing, two of the three people responded and said that they accepted the apology. But, for this author, perhaps the most interesting thing came from the experience of the third person who did not respond: even though this person didn't respond, the author still felt a huge sense of relief from a burden he had been carrying for many years. He couldn't force the person to accept the apology, nor did he ever expect the person to rekindle their friendship, but he did want the person to know that he was sorry and he was confident that the person received the message.

Building Your Practice:

- When you harm someone, the most compassionate response is to make amends.

- Making amends means feeling, facing, and acknowledging the pain you've caused rather than avoiding it. It also means atoning for your actions, doing the best you can to help relieve—or to prevent—suffering.

- The five steps to making amends are: (1) taking responsibility for your actions, (2) deciding on the conditions and content of how you are going to make amends, (3) creating intentions without any expectations, (4) making an atonement, and (5) making amends regularly.

- In addition, keep using Deep Knowledge Meditation as situations arise that require wise choices.

- Also, continue your Morning Intentions to recognize the moments of choice, and identify the opportunities during the day to enact your values-based intentions. When barriers arise, use your "Barriers Log" to plan a way through.

Chapter 12

Impermanence

If you had to answer the question "What is the root cause of suffering in the world?" what would your answer be? Think about it for a few seconds and try. Many people would say "money" or "the love of power." Others might suggest one of the Seven Deadly Sins: gluttony, lust, greed, pride, anger, envy, and laziness. And still others would have their own answers. In some ways, each of these answers would be accurate some of the time. But is there a universal root cause that underlies each of these answers?

Approximately 2500 years ago, a young man in northern India sat under the shade of a tree to think about this same question. He is reported to have sat there thinking about the question for forty-nine days in quiet meditation before he finally figured out the answer. It is said that when this young man discovered the origin of suffering he became enlightened—meaning spiritually aware or spiritually awake—and so his followers referred to him as "Buddha" meaning the "enlightened one."

Now, we are not suggesting that you have to become a Buddhist to understand the nature of suffering, nor do you have to become a Buddhist to become more spiritually aware. But the answer that the young man discovered is hard to argue with: suffering occurs when you fail to realize that all things are *impermanent*. The truth is that nothing lasts forever or stays the same forever. All things die, change, or fade away. But when we grasp onto something and try to make it last forever—or demand that it remain the same forever—we eventually become sad, angry, disappointed, or hurt when that thing disappears or changes. And this leads to suffering.

This applies to everything. Our emotional states of happiness and sadness don't last forever—they eventually fade and change—and our physical state doesn't remain healthy forever—we all go through cycles of health and sickness throughout our lives and eventually we die. Nothing truly lasts forever. You can fight this fact and get angry or sad about it, but that doesn't change the truth that nothing in the physical world is permanent. All physical things are forever changing.

Now, some might say that "God is eternal" or "Your soul never dies," and we agree with that. Many *nonphysical* things do last forever, like the All, the Creator or God; your soul; and your relationships with all the souls you've ever loved. If you believe in reincarnation, the knowledge, wisdom, and values that you learn are never lost, only forgotten for a little while. Love, consciousness, and truth are also all eternal.

But these are spiritual things, not physical things. The spiritual world *is* eternal, and that is why we have encouraged you to connect with your spiritual values and spiritually focused actions in this workbook. The physical world, on the other hand, is impermanent; it decays, changes, and disappears. So when you place sole responsibility for your happiness in something that is impermanent—something of the physical world—and neglect what is spiritual and permanent in your life—like love, your values, and your connection to spirit—you often become disappointed and suffer when those physical things change.

Impermanence Does Not Mean Lack of Caring

Impermanence is a difficult concept to accept. The idea of impermanence is threatening to many. It's hard to think about our loved ones dying, our own deaths, our possessions disappearing, or our relationships ending. And as a result, much confusion about impermanence has occurred. Some people have equated impermanence with a state of "not caring" or "not trying." They believe that in order to accept the fact that all things will die or fade away they also have to stop caring, stop loving, or stop getting involved in relationships.

But that is far from the truth. An acceptance of impermanence does not mean that you also have to become uncaring toward others or indifferent toward circumstances in life. In fact, a true acceptance of impermanence requires the complete opposite response:

to truly care about someone or something *and accept that the person or thing will someday not be there* requires an extraordinary amount of love.

Imagine how your relationships would be different if you simultaneously acknowledged that you loved someone and accepted the fact that they would one day disappear from your life, either because of death or because of some form of disconnection. How much more important and precious might that person appear to you, knowing that the time you have with him or her is limited? How much more attention would you pay to that person? How much more intently would you listen to what he or she has to say? How much more important would your interactions with that person be? The general answer to these questions is: "A lot!" An acceptance of impermanence tends to heighten your experience of everyday moments in life, as well as your appreciation for things you think are important. Since you can never guarantee that there will ever be another moment like this one—whatever it is that you're doing—you'll tend to value it more.

So, again, if you accept the fact that all things are impermanent, it doesn't mean that you also have to stop caring, stop falling in love, or stop forming relationships with other people. However, it does mean that you stop attaching your sole happiness or complete personal success to other people, things, or circumstances that you hope will remain static, positive, or alive *forever*. Because all physical things are impermanent, including the best people, the happiest relationships, the most joyous emotions, and the most favorable circumstances. The key to succeeding in a world of impermanence is to love others as much as you can, to engage with life fully using your spiritual values as a guide, and to appreciate what you have in your life—all while simultaneously accepting that everything changes and eventually disappears. This, obviously, is very hard to do, and it takes effort. (Later in this chapter, you'll be introduced to a mindfulness exercise and some other suggestions to help you incorporate an acceptance of impermanence into your life.)

Pain Versus Suffering

Now, with a basic understanding of impermanence, let's discuss the difference between pain and suffering. If you go back and reread this chapter, you'll notice that we have been talking about the cause of "suffering," not of "pain." That's because there is a difference. The word "pain" comes from the same Latin root as the word "penalty." In a sense, pain is like a penalty when something hurts you. Pain is usually acute, meaning it happens immediately after an injury but eventually disappears. Suffering, on the other hand, comes from the Latin root words meaning "to carry." In some ways, suffering implies pain that is *prolonged* because it is carried forward. So when we discuss "clinging to permanence" or "attachment to permanence" as being the root cause of suffering, we mean that those things cause *prolonged* sorrow, torment, or distress.

Obviously, there is no escaping pain in life. There are going to be things that hurt you, both physically and emotionally. If someone steps on your toes, it will cause temporary physical pain. And if someone close to you dies, or an important relationship ends prematurely, this too will cause a period of emotional pain. However, suffering occurs when we continue to cling to the belief that those things *should not* have happened or attach ourselves to the belief that our health or our relationships *should not* have ended and *should* have remained perfect and happy forever.

In the Buddhist philosophy, there is a famous parable that illustrates this point. It is the story of a woman whose only son died at a young age. The woman was grief stricken by her loss and she suffered greatly, wondering why such a terrible thing should have happened to her son. Someone told her that an enlightened teacher, the Buddha, was in a nearby village, and the woman was encouraged to ask him for help. So the woman ran to the nearby village and pleaded with the Buddha to give her the medicine that would bring her son back to life. The Buddha saw that she was suffering greatly and understood how desperately she wanted her son back. So the Buddha told her that he would help her, but first she would have to collect a handful of mustard seeds from the other people in the village. The woman was eager to start, but then the Buddha added, "You can only collect mustard seeds from families that have never experienced the death of a loved one." So the woman desperately raced from home to home, knocking on doors, asking for mustard seeds, but then also remembering to ask if anyone had ever died in the person's family. She knocked on every door in the village, but every family had experienced the death of a family member or someone they loved. So the grieving mother was not able to collect a single mustard seed. Instead, she sat and watched the sun set and the village go dark in the stillness of the night. And at that point she too realized what the Buddha had learned sitting underneath the tree: all things are impermanent and the more you struggle against this truth, the greater you will suffer. And at that point, it is said that her suffering was lifted.

What About Happiness?

So the good news is that all unpleasant emotions are impermanent. Feelings like anger, sadness, and nervousness all eventually fade away. (They might return, obviously, as in the case of depression. But even in cases of clinical depression or generalized anxiety, there are always moments of contentment or ease, even if they are very subtle or short-lived.) Unfortunately, however, the other news is that pleasant emotions like happiness, joy, and contentment also change and disappear. No one is truly "happy all the time." The truth is, we all go through cycles of emotions and eventually return to neutral. We then remain in a neutral state of equilibrium until some stimulus acts on us again, and then we feel an emotion until it too fades away and we return to neutral again. Disappointment and suffering often occur when people think they should remain happy "all the time," or when they resist feeling sad or angry because they think "I should never feel upset." Again, the truth is, we all go through cycles of emotions in our lives, but if left alone, our emotions fade—even the happy ones—and that's okay.

Do your best to simply be mindful and aware of your emotions. Recognize that they too are impermanent. Whatever it is that is giving you joy will eventually disappear, so be mindful of it, appreciate it, enjoy the pleasure that it brings to you, but don't cling to it and try to make it something that it is not. Do not expect to feel *only* joy and happiness forever. Whatever it is that is bringing you pleasure will someday stop causing you to feel that way, or will cause you to feel something other than pleasure—either when it disappears or when your nervous system gets habituated to the stimulus and gets bored by it. For example, other people in your life will bring you joy, but eventually your relationships with them will also cause disappointment. That's normal. Your favorite possessions can also bring you joy, but they too are impermanent and will wear out, break, or disappear and cause you disappointment. So, appreciate the persons and possessions in your life. Recognize that when they disappear or die, that there will be pain, loss, and sorrow. But recognize also that acute pain will likely fade over time if you resist clinging to the belief that the physical world should be permanent. Remember that our spiritual connections are eternal even if our physical bodies are not. Living a mindful life in which you accept impermanence can deepen your emotional experiences, because there is an awareness that this moment, this person, or this possession is special because it is temporary.

Accepting impermanence in the physical world is *not* the same as saying that there is no joy in the world, nor happiness, nor positive relationships. But it does mean not attaching yourself to the hope that any of these things will last forever. Therefore, be in the present moment and enjoy it while it is occurring! Because it might not be there tomorrow.

In the next chapter, you'll learn about something else that is permanent: grace. Grace is not a gift from God, nor is it something that can be earned; rather, it is a form of happiness that can't be taken away from you by anyone or anything. Grace is a state of peace in which you live according to your spiritual values. It is the only thing and the only state of being that we have power to hold on to regardless of the situation or circumstances. We hold grace entirely by our own choices and actions. Grace is *the new happiness* that nothing can take away.

Impermanence Meditation

The purpose of this meditation is to help you become more aware of the impermanence of all physical things. This meditation is emotionally challenging. It should only be attempted after you've become comfortable practicing Still Mind Meditation for several weeks. Begin each Impermanence Meditation with the basic Still Mind Meditation technique, then use one of the suggested topics below for contemplation. Either read through each meditation before beginning, in order to familiarize yourself with the suggested images, or record the instructions on your smartphone using a slow, soothing pace.

After you have used each of the Impermanence Meditation examples below, feel free to create your own impermanence visualizations. Or, go somewhere to observe the process of impermanence in real life. For example, go to a field and watch the clouds change or sit on the beach and watch the sands shift.

Still Mind Meditation

To begin, find a quiet place where you won't be disturbed for ten to fifteen minutes. Then find a comfortable position to sit or lie down. If you have continued to use a talisman to focus your breathing and your thoughts, continue to do so. Otherwise, begin to focus on the rising and falling of your breath. Think to yourself, "Slow breath in," and allow your stomach to release and expand like a balloon as you slowly inhale. Then think to yourself, "Slow breath out," and allow your stomach to gently deflate as you slowly exhale. Continue to take several slow breaths in and slow breaths out, allowing both your body and mind to relax and slow down. *(Pause here.)*

Impermanence Meditation Suggestions

Weather and seasons. Imagine yourself sitting in a beautiful, peaceful meadow lined with trees. You are completely safe and at peace. Here, you can be still and just watch the sky and the trees without being disturbed. As you sit, you begin to notice the clouds in the sky. At first, they appear to be unchanging, but as you continue to watch them, you notice that they are slowly gathering and growing. There is a slight breeze pushing the clouds along. Ever so slightly, the clouds are changing, first they grow, and then as the breeze continues to push them in the sky, they change form, break up, and begin to disappear. They are never the same, they are always in a state of movement and change, even if it is happening slowly. Continue to watch the clouds get pushed along by the breeze, changing form, and eventually disappearing. *(Pause here.)* Then, too, notice the movement of the sun arcing across the sky. Its movement is never static, it never stops in its path across the sky. As the planet continues to rotate, the sun moves ever so slightly from one side of the horizon to the other. Notice the color of the grass and the colors of the trees in the distance as they change with the fading light. *(Pause here.)* Now imagine the movement of the sun speeding up and completing its journey to the west, and then imagine the moon rising, casting its glow on the meadow. Notice how the landscape changes appearance again in the soft light of the moon. Notice how the clouds, grass, and trees all change in appearance. *(Pause here.)* Do your best to continue watching the movement of the clouds, the sun, and the moon as they move across the sky, each of them constantly changing. Then imagine the landscape changing further as the seasons change from summer, to fall, to winter, and to spring. The leaves of the trees turn colors, fall off, get covered in snow, and then new leaves appear in the spring thaw. Continue imagining this changing scenery of weather and time and notice the subtle ways in which nature displays its impermanence.

Shifting stream. Imagine yourself sitting beside a beautiful stream or river. You are completely safe and at peace. Here you can be still and just watch the water flowing past. As you sit, you begin to notice where the ripples form in the movement of the water and you notice the sound of the water moving past you. The water is in constant motion and ever changing. As you observe it longer, you begin to notice that each ripple and splash of water is unique, no two are ever exactly the same. So too with the sound of the water, it all sounds similar, but as you listen longer you start to notice that the melody of the sound changes very subtly. As you continue to observe, you also notice the leaves, sticks, and flecks of foam that are being carried by the water. Each of them is unique as well. No two look exactly the same, and therefore the stream or river itself is changing appearance and form every second. The stream or river is never the same.

Life of a seed. Imagine yourself sitting somewhere relaxing and calm. You are completely safe and at peace. Wherever you are, in front of you is a clear glass container filled with soil and nutrients. And planted in the container is a magical flower seed that grows as quickly as you want it to. Imagine yourself sprinkling the soil with water. The seed awakens and begins to grow. Through the container you can see the seed split open and a tiny white root began to sprout. The root grows thicker and longer. And as the main root grows farther down into the soil, more tiny roots begin to sprout from it. Then suddenly a green stem begins to push up through the earth, looking for the light of the sun. The stem takes the husk of the shell with it, until it pushes through the soil and then casts the husk aside. Magically, the roots below the soil continue to branch off and begin to fill the glass vessel. Above the soil, the stem of the flower grows taller and thicker. Then the tiny bud of a flower appears. Quickly the bud grows plump, and tiny green leaves take shape below it. The stem grows taller in the sunlight and then suddenly the bud begins to open, revealing bright, brilliantly colored petals. The glass vessel is now filled with roots, and the flower has reached its fully mature height. The petals of the flower are now fully open and turn to face the sun. As the sun arcs across the sky, the face of the flower follows the path. A honey bee flies into the flower and collects pollen on its body that it will spread to other flowers, causing new seeds to grow. But now, as the sun starts to descend, the flower begins to wilt. And as the sky goes dark, the petals of the flower fall off, the stem turns brown, and the flower dies. Finally, the roots, stem, and petals fully decay, returning to the soil, and provide nutrients for the next seed to be planted. Be mindful that all living things grow, die, and decay. All living things change. All living things are impermanent. And as something old ends, something new begins. There is no good or bad, only change.

Thoughts, feelings, and emotions. After getting centered with Still Mind Meditation, simply be silent and observe. Notice your thoughts as they arise and change, moment by moment. Do your best not to get attached to them, simply notice them as they are created by your brain. Each day your brain produces millions of thoughts. Some of them are important, and some of them are not. Some of them deserve your attention, but many of them do not. Do your best just to observe your thoughts without getting attached to them. Just as a fish will sometimes pass a piece of bait secured to a fishing hook, do your best not to "bite" on the thoughts that arise. Simply note, *There's a thought*, or *I'm thinking*, and then imagine the thought floating away on a cloud or a balloon. Do your best to observe the impermanent, ever-changing state of your thoughts without getting attached to any one particular thought. Simply observe the process of thinking. *(Pause here.)* Now do the same with your physical feelings and sensations. Scan your body from your toes to your head, mentally observing every inch of your body for physical sensations such as an itch, pain, pressure, temperature, or muscle tightness. Again, just notice and say to yourself, *I'm feeling* or *There's a sensation*. Do not attach yourself to the feeling. Notice it and observe it. Notice if it changes, moves, shifts, or disappears. Do not try to fix it. Just observe it, then continue scanning other areas of your body. Notice how your physical feelings are frequently changing in intensity, location, and type. *(Pause here.)* Now turn your attention to your emotional state. For some, it might help to focus on the solar plexus or heart areas of the body. Notice how you are feeling emotionally. Positive or negative? Good or bad? Happy? Sad? Irritable? Whatever it is, do your best to just notice without judging and without trying to figure out why. Even if you can't name it, just notice it. Observe your emotional state for a few minutes, and notice any changes to it, no matter how subtle. Perhaps it rises or falls in intensity. Or maybe it changes completely. Again, don't actively try to change it or alter it. Just observe the way your emotions rise, fall, change, and disappear.

Act with Impermanence

Now that you have an idea of what impermanence is, and hopefully have some experience mindfully observing impermanence, the next task is to incorporate impermanence into your life—in a sense, to act *with* impermanence. Think of it like a partnership. You can do whatever you want in life, but your partner "impermanence" is always there to remind you that nothing lasts forever—not even you. So, begin to ask yourself how impermanence influences your values, your spiritual actions, and your daily behaviors. For example, you might want to review your values in chapter 2 and question whether or not impermanence affects the things that are important to you. In light of this new information, are there things that now seem more precious? Or less precious? Consider modifying your values if necessary. Do the same with your moment of choice decisions and your life purpose, and maybe even review the last chapter to determine if there is anyone else to whom you now need to make amends. Use the space below to identify any modifications in your values, your values-based choices, your life purpose, or needed amends as you view them through the lens of impermanence.

_____

_____

_____

_____

_____

_____

_____

_____

In general, throughout your daily life, try to remember that each day, every event, and all the people you love are extremely valuable because there is no way to predict when they will cease to be here physically. For some people, acting with impermanence might also mean that they stop procrastinating and begin doing the things they really want to do—including taking nonharmful risks or stepping beyond their comfort zone into activities that they've previously avoided. Because who knows what the future holds? Use the space below to identify any actions you've been putting off and might want to consider doing now.

_____

_____

_____

_____

_____

_____

_____

_____

_____

Acting with impermanence might also mean that you reevaluate your relationships with certain people. Consider the closest people in your life and ask yourself what you might miss most about each of them if they should suddenly disappear from your life. Then further ask yourself if you need to strengthen, alter, or reaffirm any of those relationships. Do you need to validate certain people to let them know that your relationship with them is extremely important? Hopefully, acting with impermanence will also encourage you to be fully present in the moment with the people you love and care about. Consider that your time with them here is limited, so while you're with them, do your best to focus on them rather than thinking about or doing other things. Or maybe the opposite is true: in light of the fact that all things are impermanent, maybe you also need to consider eliminating certain people or activities from your life that drain you or are harmful to you. Use the space below to list the ways that your awareness of impermanence might change your key relationships.

_____

_____

_____

_____

_____

Hopefully, acting with impermanence will also encourage you to take better care of yourself—body, mind, and spirit. We can all do a better job in some ways of healthier eating, exercising more, and getting rid of stress, so why continue to put it off? Consider making healthier choices for yourself. Use the concept of impermanence to prioritize your life. Ask yourself, "What's really important?" Imagine if you knew that you were going to die tomorrow, what would you want to spend your final hours doing? Figure it out and make those things your immediate priorities in life while you are still alive. Use the space below to prioritize your actions for a healthy life in light of your impermanence.

_____

_____

_____

_____

_____

_____

_____

Building Your Practice:

- Nothing in the physical world is permanent; all things are in fact *impermanent*.

- The root cause of suffering is failing to recognize that all things are impermanent and attaching yourself to the faulty belief that some things will never change, fade away, or die.

- Use the Impermanence Meditation to remind yourself about the short-lived nature of the physical world.

- Some spiritual elements like love, wisdom, and truth *are* eternal; therefore, allow them to inform your values, your daily actions, and your priorities in life.

- Continue using Deep Knowledge Meditation as situations arise that require wise choices.

- Also, continue your Morning Intentions to recognize the moments of choice, and identify the opportunities during the day to enact your values-based intentions. When barriers arise, use your "Barriers Log" to plan a way through.

Chapter 13

Finding a State of Grace

In the last chapter, you explored what you cannot control and cannot keep. As the Buddhists tell us, most everything is impermanent. It will fade, break, or be lost. Time erodes even the greatest monuments and the greatest empires. All will disappear. But, as you learned, there is one thing that cannot be taken from us while we live. It is grace, a form of happiness in which you live according to your spiritual values. Grace can be felt in everything you do.

Understanding Grace

There's no universal pathway to grace, no right road. Grace is something you give yourself. It is created by your own actions, a product of every choice that is aligned with your unique values and mission. Grace is a form of happiness that can't be taken away by anyone or anything. It can only be diminished—temporarily—by choices that distance you from your purpose and mission.

Subjectively, grace is experienced as a sense of peace, an inner quiet. Some people use the word contentment. Though you may face losses and hurts, though things you counted on may be taken away, though goals you sought may slip out of your grasp, that sense of peace can remain at the very core of your life. You may be scared, you may be sad, you may have physical pain, yet grace can continue like a low, reassuring murmur right alongside every struggle. As long as your actions flow from what truly matters, from why you are here, you will have grace.

What Grace Is Not

Grace isn't an emotion. Emotions come and go; we have dozens each day. The happiest, most light-hearted emotion dissipates. Grace isn't joy. The joy of being in the flow, completely immersed in the present moment, is also ephemeral. As soon as you feel threatened or worried, as soon as you leave the present to solve a problem, the flow is gone. The joy is a memory.

Grace is not a gift from God. Grace isn't earned by following religious rules or dogma. It is not achieved by denying yourself things you desire or stripping pleasure from your life. Grace is not "being good."

Your Practices—A Pathway to Grace

Grace, as we've said, comes from our choices and actions. But so many of our choices are automatic, driven by pain and the avoidance of pain. Choices aligned with purpose and mission can easily be forgotten. Or we may not even notice that the choice exists. Spiritual practices, such as the ones you've learned in this book, help us see past the moments of pain and suffering to the reason we are here. They help us make values-based choices and, ultimately, create a pathway to grace.

The practices most useful for generating a state of grace are Still Mind Meditation, Compassion Meditation, Deep Knowledge Meditation, the Morning Intention, and Acceptance Meditation.

Still Mind Meditation. Still Mind Meditation teaches you to notice the present moment, to be aware of now. It's not just about watching your breath; it's about noticing what's happening inside of you, seeing your emotions, your pain, and your impulses. It will also help you see the moment where you can choose how to respond according to your values.

Seeing the moment of choice and linking it to your core spiritual values infuses grace into your life.

Laura has been doing Still Mind Meditation for about three months. Initially, her mind produced a lot of intrusive thoughts while she tried to watch her breath. That's happening less now, but what's more important is that she's seeing what's occurring in the moment. When, for example, her husband decided to take a lengthy business trip, she noticed her sadness, a painful, lonely feeling, and an impulse to say something angry. She also noticed judgmental thoughts such as: *He doesn't make time for his family.* Laura was able to watch every part of her experience and realize that she didn't have to act on either her emotional urges or her judgmental thoughts. She could plainly see other choices based on her spiritual values, and by acting on them she created a life of inner peace, contentment, and grace.

Compassion Meditation. Compassion is seeing the truth that we all suffer and struggle, that we all have difficult emotions and sometimes make choices that cause pain to ourselves and others. Compassion lies at the root of all relationships, allowing us to see the humanity in each other and the beautiful, flawed humanness in our own being. Without compassion, it's easy to treat people as objects, as something other, or as something unworthy. Without compassion, we can reject ourselves as bad or wrong or undeserving.

The Compassion for Others Meditation strengthens your awareness of, and ability to act on, service values. The Self-Compassion Meditation strengthens your personal growth values and the ability to act on those intentions. These meditations will help you focus on living a life based on caring for yourself and others—and fill you with a sense of grace.

Anthony had an easier time feeling compassion for others than for himself. From childhood, he'd carried a sense of unworthiness and endured a lot of self-critical thoughts. When he began to include the Self-Compassion Meditation among his practices, the words seemed rote rather than felt. Even worse, they sometimes seemed false and triggered a self-attack. But Anthony kept at his daily practice, using Still Mind Meditation, Compassion for Others Meditation, and Self-Compassion Meditation. He sought to recognize that he was a person who struggled and felt pain, and he wanted to feel some form of happiness.

Sticking to his daily practice over a period of several months, two things happened that surprised Anthony. First, he found that he was more willing to act on self-care intentions regarding exercise and healthy food. Second, he noticed that the self-critical thoughts seemed to be less frequent. His new ability to act on self-care values strengthened his sense of grace.

Deep Knowledge Meditation. The process of sourcing your own wisdom, or getting help from Spirit, is an important way you turn values into action. It creates grace because it is the means by which abstract principles (values) become real choices. Life on this planet keeps confronting us with threats and losses and mountains to climb. On a personal level, each day has multiple decisions that require a wise response to someone else's anger, judgment, disappointment, or needs. There's no end to situations where our emotions and pain push us in one direction and our values and mission pull us in another. The practice of Deep Knowledge Meditation, as you face these daily choices, is how you remember what matters.

Glenda's use of Deep Knowledge Meditation evolved over time. At first, she tried it when she was upset (primarily with her boyfriend) and she needed to access her own wisdom for how to deal with his demands and her feelings of hurt. Over and over, the meditation sparked a strong sense that she had to tell her truth, acknowledging her feelings and needs to a man who wasn't good at hearing them.

Later, Glenda began using Deep Knowledge Meditation to help her recognize what was important in terms of her life mission. Her work as a court reporter began to seem less important, and the meditations drew her attention to a nearby childcare center specializing in handicapped toddlers. At first she volunteered, and later decided to go back to school for a certificate in Early Childhood Education. Accessing her wisdom led to a career change, and eventually a paying job at the center where she'd once been a volunteer. Her sense of recognizing and acting on her values gave her a new sense of grace.

The Morning Intention. The Morning Intention, as you've learned to use it, creates grace in three ways. First, it can remind you to notice the moments of choice—when pain or high emotion might push you away from your spiritual values. Second, the Morning Intention can serve to remind you of your mission—that single statement of purpose that illuminates each moment of your day. Third, it can bring your attention to a small list of values-based goals for the next twenty-four hours.

Joseph never told anyone his life mission because it seemed embarrassingly simple, perhaps even sounding a bit idealistic: it was to love everyone he encountered. His Moment of Choice Intention was simple, too—to act with love, even when hurt or upset. And he made a list of situations each morning (mostly anticipated meetings or encounters) where he planned to express love—by giving praise, support, encouragement, attention, and so on. The Morning Intention, for Joseph, was a major pathway to grace.

Acceptance Meditation. The Acceptance Meditation is about facing pain—both difficult emotions and paralyzing thoughts—that get in the way of doing the things that matter. These barriers to spiritual values can hijack your mission and temporarily disrupt the peace that comes from grace. Acceptance means making room for all the hammering thoughts that tell you to stop trying or to give up because it won't work. And to allow feelings of fear and discouragement—even despair—to manifest themselves while still doing your Daily Intentions.

Miranda did the Acceptance Meditation daily. It was part of her practice. And it meant something special because the meditation strengthened her ability to face her father's progressive dementia. Miranda's father remained in his home with a caregiver, but he no longer recognized her, and was often irritable as he sought to comprehend what was going on around him. Visits were painful—full of loss and foreboding thoughts about what was to come. The caregiver reported problems and kept hinting that her father was a "handful" and might "need to be placed."

The meditation helped Miranda soften and make room for grief, and to accept the anxious thoughts about when and how her father might have to leave his home. As each difficult thought arose, Miranda just allowed it and soothed herself with a gentle breath. The words "soften, hold, let be" came to her frequently while visiting her father, and with those words was a sense of calmness, of grace. She was acting on her values of care and support; she kept showing up despite her worry and sadness.

Returning to Grace

The calm contentment of grace will grow and diminish, strengthen and fade over and over during the course of your life. This happens as we walk closer or farther from the path set by our values and mission. Notice your state of grace, notice the strength of your alignment with spiritual values. When that sense of grace diminishes, you can bring it back. It is always within your power to recommit to your mission, to your values, and to your purpose. The means are at hand: your practices plus the willingness to face the emotional and mental barriers that often stand between you and doing the things that matter.

Building Your Practice:

- Grace is a form of deep contentment that diminishes when the things you do aren't in alignment with the things you care about. You make your own state of grace by acting on values and life mission.

- Grace is something you give yourself with the choices you make every day.

- Spiritual practices that generate grace include Still Mind Meditation, Compassion Meditation, Deep Knowledge Meditation, Morning Intentions, and Acceptance Meditation.

- Set time aside each day for your practices. You might do some in the morning—for example, the Still Mind and Compassion Meditations with your Morning Intentions. At some other quiet time, you might do the Deep Knowledge and Acceptance Meditations. The period reserved for your practices should ideally be the same, day after day.

Chapter 14

Bringing Spirit to Your Daily Life

Spirituality is so much more than the belief in something—even the belief in your values and mission. True spirituality is rooted in what you *do*; the choices and actions you make each day. Your life is your creative spiritual act. Your choices—every moment—bring spirit into the world. They give spirit a face and hands. Turning spirit into daily action is how you grow and how spirit lives.

Your key to success in the future will depend on your continuing to make choices based on your values. Simply put, the more consistent your choices are with your values, the more fulfilling your life will become, despite whatever hurts and losses may occur along the way. Conversely, the more inconsistent your choices are with your values, the less fulfilling your life will seem. The practices you've learned in this book are the means by which you align choices and actions with your mission and values.

The two kinds of practices you've learned here are *awareness practices* and *action practices*. Awareness practices help you see the spiritual choices in daily life. Action practices turn choices into actual deeds. We'll review them here. And while you're reading through, put a check mark next to each practice that you use twice or more each week.

Awareness Practices

☐ Still Mind Meditation: focusing on your breath while noticing and letting go of thoughts.

☐ Still Mind Meditation plus Compassion Meditation: focusing on your breath, then on compassionate intentions for peace and happiness—both for others and for yourself.

☐ Deep Knowledge Meditation: seeking awareness for a wise choice—either internally or in the world of spirit.

☐ Acceptance Meditation: seeking acceptance of the pain that often shows up as we act on mission and values.

☐ "Moment of Choice Journal": reviewing outcomes of each moment of choice throughout the day when pain, strong emotions, or strong desires show up.

☐ Missed Moment of Choice Visualization: after taking an action not aligned with your mission or values, you visualize the scene and mentally rehearse a different, values-based action.

Action Practices

☐ Morning Intention: reviewing your "Life Mission Statement" and identifying likely moments/opportunities throughout the day to act on mission/values.

☐ Moment of Choice: recognizing the moment of choice as it occurs and choosing values-based actions.

☐ Amends: whenever an action or choice harms another, acknowledging what was done and making some form of amends as soon as possible.

Your Long-Term Spiritual Action Plan

Briefly review the practices you did *not* check. Are any of these worthy of reconsideration, even if it means experimenting for a week to see if they help you get more aligned with your values and mission? If you want to reconsider a practice, commit to doing it for the next week. Now it's time to make your "Long-Term Spiritual Action Plan." This plan will include *all* the awareness and action practices you are committed to using at least twice a week (preferably more). On the following worksheet, write the practices you are committing to in the boxes that head each column (under Practice 1, Practice 2, etc.). Duplicate the page so you can monitor use of your practices over several months (until the practices become positive habits that you do automatically).

This kind of monitoring process greatly increases the likelihood that your chosen practices will become an everyday (or most days) part of your life. Checking each one you use on any given date keeps you aware of your commitment and also helps you notice which practices are used less frequently or are falling out of your spiritual repertoire. (You can download a PDF of the action plan at http://www.newharbinger.com/43379.)

Long-Term Spiritual Action Plan

(Make an effort to practice your skills and review your mission statement regularly.)

DATE	PRACTICE						
	1	2	3	4	5	6	7
Sat. 12/06	✓	✓	✓	✓	✓	✓	✓

Example: Renee's Long-Term Plan

Renee works as a paralegal in a firm that does family law—divorces, prenuptials, and separation agreements. Her job mostly entails gathering information about assets and income. She doesn't much care for the job, but it's a decent living for herself and her eight-year-old daughter. Renee's family was Episcopalian, but she got turned off from religion in Sunday school, and her practices have been limited to an occasional prayer for her daughter (who suffers with asthma). For years, Renee has felt a chronic lethargy, as if she struggled to put one foot in front of the other. Her life has been a string of necessary tasks punctuated by a few hours of cable TV at night. She occasionally goes on a date, but socializing is restricted to every other weekend when her daughter stays with Renee's ex-husband.

As Renee started to explore the practices in this book, she found that Still Mind Meditation seemed to calm her and help her be a little more observant about her life. When she combined Still Mind Meditation with journaling her moments of choice and noticing whether choices were values-based, Renee began to see something changing. Her life was starting to become more conscious. She was noticing what she did and didn't do and how strong emotions, pain, or desire impacted her choices.

Renee had a problem at work (a litigated divorce where her research on the family's assets was harshly challenged in court) and lost track of her new practices. A few weeks later, she had a fight with her daughter. It was ugly and angry, and she realized it wouldn't have happened if she had been alert to the moment of choice. Renee returned to her practices, and began to work further into the program.

The Compassion Meditation seemed quirky and rote to her. After a week of trying, she couldn't get past the feeling that she was reciting the kind of prayers she learned in Sunday school. On the other hand, Deep Knowledge Meditation made Renee feel in touch with the wisest parts of herself. Along with her Morning Intention, she used it to sort out challenging situations that might come up that day.

The Acceptance Meditation felt comforting to Renee, but on a deeper level, she knew it was teaching her something she needed to learn: how to allow and not resist things beyond her control; how to accept the pain that often accompanies acting on values.

For example, Renee sometimes felt boredom listening to her daughter talk endlessly about her day in the third grade. But she was learning to accept the feeling so she could act on her values of kindness and paying attention. Sometimes Renee struggled with fear of judgment and failure regarding a children's book she was trying to write. Yet she was also learning to accept these feelings as inevitable and unavoidable if she was going to live her value of creativity.

Renee never tried the Missed Moment of Choice Visualization. It seemed too complicated, and she was getting better and better at catching moments of choice without it. She let it go, knowing she didn't have to do everything. She could focus instead on practices that were appealing and worked for her.

The action practices were the most motivating for Renee. She had identified a life mission (supporting people in need) and five key values (kindness, paying attention/understanding, creativity, learning, and protecting). Every day—at work, with her daughter, and with friends—she looked for opportunities to act with kindness and understanding. She put extra effort into advising and supporting clients in the law office who were distressed by the divorce process, or who had suffered trauma in their marriage. Renee turned her value of learning into an online counseling course and another on domestic violence. She became the office expert on mental health resources for abused women.

Her job now felt different because she had woven her spiritual values into it. And her experience as a parent also changed because the commitment to understanding and protecting had made her relationship to her daughter sweeter and more engaged. Renee made amends quickly if she said something hurtful—whether it was to her daughter or to her ex-husband (there was friction in their co-parenting relationship).

For Renee, the outcomes from her spiritual growth were very noticeable. The sadness and lethargy that had marked her life diminished. In their place was a new happiness that felt like a sense of peace, of contentment.

Renee wanted to keep what she'd gained, and to stay focused on her spiritual values and mission. To do so, her long-term plan included these daily practices:

- Still Mind Meditation

- Acceptance Meditation

- Morning Intention: remembering her mission and anticipating opportunities to act on mission and values throughout the day.

- Deep Knowledge Meditation

- Noticing moments of choice and acting on values (she stopped doing the "Moment of Choice Journal" after a while, finding it unnecessary).

- Making amends.

Practices Versus Beliefs

Every religion and spiritual tradition has a cosmology—beliefs and ideas about the origin of the universe, why we are here, the nature of the divine, and what is good or bad. These beliefs help some people feel that they can get a glimpse of "truth," that they can see past death and all the suffering on this planet to how things really work.

But unfortunately, no one knows which of these beliefs is 100 percent true. They can be reassuring, but we hold them all on faith, with no guarantees or certainty. Religious and spiritual *practices* are another matter. These were developed to make our lives better, and we can evaluate them to see if they're true. The nine practices in this book—those supporting both awareness and values-based action—grow from multiple spiritual traditions. They have helped many people find their spiritual path and live a life of grace—the happiness that comes from alignment with our deepest values.

As you've learned and utilized these practices, you have tested them to see if they work for you. Some have helped you live closer to grace, bringing your life and your choices nearer to your values and mission. Some may not have been useful for you. That's only to be expected. Practices aren't a rule book that you blindly follow. Practices are paths to spirit—some will work for you and some won't. Your mission now is to keep using the practices that lead you toward love, toward values, and toward spirit. And to use them as often as you can—daily, if possible.

The spiritual practices you have learned will bring you to a life no longer shaped by issues of pleasure and pain, and no longer focused on satiety or relief from suffering. Rather, the practices will lead you through your life with a compass setting grounded in your own truth, with your own sense of what matters, and in your own relationship to spirit.

Your Journey from Here

Each of us has our own core values and our own mission. As your choices align with these, you begin to feel a deep and enduring grace. Where you go from here—your spiritual path—will be unique to you. But the practices you've learned, if you continue them, will keep Spirit alive—in you and through you. Mark Twain once said that the two most important days in people's lives are the day they're born and the day they find out why.

You have been learning *why*. And your work is to keep remembering it.

A Note for Therapists

The New Happiness draws on Acceptance and Commitment Therapy principles—establishing values, developing mindfulness, and committing to acceptance—to help readers develop a personal path to spiritual growth and lasting happiness. The authors are pleased to offer therapists a free ten-week protocol for a Post-Trauma Growth and Wisdom group incorporating these principles and many of the practices found in this book.

Visit http://www.newharbinger.com/43379 to download this resource.

References

Amin, M., M. Maroufi, and M. Sadeghi. 2017. The effectiveness of ACT on psychological, social, and spiritual health of the patients with angina pectoris. *International Journal of Educational and Psychological Resources* 3: 240-244.

Baer, R. A. 2003. Mindfulness training as a clinical intervention: A conceptual and empirical review. *Clinical Psychology: Science and Practice* 10: 125-143.

Dworsky, C. K. O., K. I. Pargament, S. Wong, and J. J. Exline. 2016. Suppressing spiritual struggles: The role of experiential avoidance in mental health. *Journal of Contextual Behavioral Science* 5: 258-265.

Germer, C., and K. Neff. Date unknown. "Soften, Soothe, Allow" meditation. https://self-compassion.org/category/exercises/#guided-meditations.

Hawkes, A. L., K. Pakenham, S. Chambers, T. Patrao, and K. Courneya. 2014. Effects of multiple health behavior change interventions for colorectal cancer survivors on psychosocial outcomes and quality of life: A randomized controlled trial. *Annals of Behavior Medicine* 48: 359-370.

Murphy, M., and S. Donovan. 1997. *The Psychological and Physiological Effects of Meditation: A Review of Contemporary Research and a Comprehensive Bibliography 1931–1996.* 2nd ed. Sausalito, CA: Institute of Noetic Studies.

Nieuwsma, J. A., R. Walser, J. Farnsworth, and W. Nash. 2015. Possibilities within acceptance and commitment therapy for approaching moral injury. *Current Psychiatry Reviews* 11: 193-206.

Nieuwsma, J. A., R. Walser, and S. C. Hayes. 2016. *ACT for clergy and pastoral counselors.* Oakland, CA: New Harbinger Publications.

Santiago, P., and T. Gall. 2016. Acceptance and commitment therapy as a spiritually integrated psychotherapy. *Counseling and Values* 61: 239-254.

Strecher, V. J. 2016. *Life on Purpose: How Living for What Matters Most Changes Everything.* New York: HarperOne.

Walsh, R., and S. Shapiro. 2006. A meeting of meditative disciplines and western psychology: A mutually enriching dialogue. *American Psychologist* 61: 227-239.

Warren. R. 2002. *The Purpose Driven Life: What on Earth Am I Here For?* Grand Rapids, MI: Zondervan.

Matthew McKay, PhD, is a professor at the Wright Institute in Berkeley, CA. He has authored and coauthored numerous books, including *The Relaxation and Stress Reduction Workbook*, *Self-Esteem*, *Thoughts and Feelings*, *ACT on Life Not on Anger*, and *Seeking Jordan*. McKay received his PhD in clinical psychology from the California School of Professional Psychology, and specializes in the treatment of post-traumatic stress disorder (PTSD) and traumatic grief. He lives and works in the greater San Francisco Bay Area.

Jeffrey C. Wood, PsyD, lives and works in Las Vegas, NV. He specializes in brief cognitive behavioral therapy (CBT); executive coaching; and guidance for spiritual development, to include hypnotic regressions. He is coauthor of *The Dialectical Behavior Therapy Skills Workbook*, and author of *The Cognitive Behavioral Therapy Workbook for Personality Disorders*. He can be reached at TheNewHappiness@yahoo.com.

Foreword writer **Steven C. Hayes, PhD**, is foundation professor in the department of psychology at the University of Nevada, Reno, and cofounder of acceptance and commitment therapy (ACT). His career has focused on an analysis of the nature of human language and cognition, and the application of this to the understanding and alleviation of human suffering and the promotion of human prosperity.

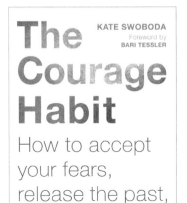

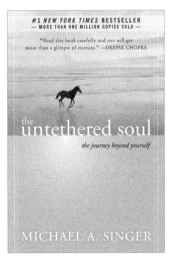

MORE TOOLS *for* POSITIVE CHANGE
by Matthew McKay *and* Jeffrey Wood

ISBN: 978-1572245136 / US $24.95

The Dialectical Behavior Therapy Skills Workbook offers evidence-based, step-by-step exercises for learning distress tolerance, mindfulness, emotion regulation, and interpersonal effectiveness and putting them to work for real and lasting change.

newharbingerpublications
1-800-748-6273 / newharbinger.com

(VISA, MC, AMEX / prices subject to change without notice)